Science Projects About
the Science
Behind Magic

Titles in the **Science Projects** *series*

**Science Fair Projects—
Planning, Presenting, Succeeding**
ISBN 0-89490-949-5

**Science Projects
About Chemistry**
ISBN 0-89490-531-7

**Science Projects
About Electricity and Magnets**
ISBN 0-89490-530-9

**Science Projects About
the Environment
and Ecology**
ISBN 0-89490-951-7

**Science Projects
About the Human Body**
ISBN 0-89490-443-4

**Science Projects About
Kitchen Chemistry**
ISBN 0-89490-953-3

**Science Projects
About Light**
ISBN 0-89490-529-5

**Science Projects
About Math**
ISBN 0-89490-950-9

**Science Projects About
Methods of Measuring**
ISBN 0-7660-1169-0

**Science Projects About
Physics in the Home**
ISBN 0-89490-948-7

**Science Projects About the
Physics of Sports**
ISBN 0-7660-1167-4

**Science Projects About the
Physics of Toys and Games**
ISBN 0-7660-1165-8

**Science Projects
About Plants**
ISBN 0-89490-952-5

**Science Projects About the
Science Behind Magic**
ISBN 0-7660-1164-X

**Science Projects About Solids,
Liquids, and Gases**
ISBN 0-7660-1168-2

**Science Projects
About Sound**
ISBN 0-7660-1166-6

**Science Projects
About Temperature
and Heat**
ISBN 0-89490-534-1

**Science Projects
About Weather**
ISBN 0-89490-533-3

Science Projects About the Science Behind Magic

Robert Gardner

Enslow Publishers, Inc.

40 Industrial Road   PO Box 38
Box 398   Aldershot
Berkeley Heights, NJ 07922   Hants GU12 6BP
USA   UK
http://www.enslow.com

Library of Congress Cataloging-in-Publication Data

Gardner, Robert, 1929–
    Science projects about the science behind magic / by Robert Gardner.
       p.   cm. — (Science projects)
    Includes bibliographical references and index.
    Summary: Explains how to perform a variety of magic tricks by using the laws of
nature, including demonstrations of air pressure, optical illusions, chemical reactions,
and more.
    ISBN 0-7660-1164-X
    1. Science projects Juvenile literature. 2. Magic tricks Juvenile literature.
[1. Science projects. 2. Magic tricks.] I. Title. II. Series: Gardner, Robert, 1929–
Science projects.
Q164.G377   2000
507' .8—dc21   99-23826
                                                           CIP

Printed in the United States of America

10 9 8 7 6 5 4 3 2 1

To Our Readers:
All Internet addresses in this book were active and appropriate when we went to press. Any
comments or suggestions can be sent by e-mail to Comments@enslow.com or to the address
on the back cover.

Illustration Credits: Enslow Publishers, Inc., pp. 13, 17, 27, 29, 38, 40, 49, 78,
110, 118; Stephen F. Delisle, pp. 16, 24, 31, 35, 36, 41, 45, 52, 69, 72, 77, 81, 84,
86, 89, 92, 94, 96, 101, 104, 105, 112, 115, 120.

Cover Illustration: Jerry McCrea (foreground); © Corel Corporation (background).

Contents

Introduction 7

1. There Is Magic in the Air 11

    1-1* A Balloon in a Bottle 13

    1-2   A Funnel That Will Not Empty 15

    1-3   A Bottle That Will Not Stop 17

    1-4* Getting a Lift with Air Pressure 19

    1-5   Air Pressure Can Be a Real Crusher 21

    1-6* A Geyser 23

    1-7* A Ping-Pong Ball That Defies Gravity 26

    1-8* A Voice-Controlled Submarine 29

    1-9* A Mysterious Pair of Balloons 31

2. Is Seeing Believing? 33

    2-1* Your Retaining Retina 34

    2-2* A Letter That Disappears 38

    2-3   The Lost Coin That Reappears with Water 40

    2-4* A Hole in Your Hand 43

    2-5* The Mysterious Die 45

    2-6   A Suspended Sausage 47

    2-7* Dragging a Circle 48

3. Magic Through Chemistry 50

    3-1* Dancing Raisins 51

    3-2* Genie in a Bottle 52

    3-3* Magic Chemical Paper 54

    3-4   Water to Dragon's Blood to Water 56

    3-5   A Bloody Hand 57

    3-6   Magical Bubbles 58

    3-7* Red, White, and Blue 59

    3-8* Magic Red to Green to Red 61

    3-9* Iron to Copper 63

*appropriate ideas for science fair project

3-10 Disappearing Ink   65
3-11*Turning Aladdin's Lamp Oil into Ink   66
3-12*Written Secrets.   67
3-13*A Flame That Jumps   71
3-14 A Blue Bottle   73

4. Magic Through Light and Through "Sticky" Water   75

4-1* An Inverted Scene   76
4-2* Upside-Down Shadow   80
4-3* Turning Words About.   83
4-4* Disappearing Glass   86
4-5* The Magic Mirror   88
4-6* Floating Steel   91
4-7 Water on a String   94
4-8* An Underwater Bulb   96

5. Magic Through Motion   98

5-1* The Switch and Twist. 100
5-2* Which Falls Faster, Light or Heavy?. 103
5-3 Newton, a Card, a Marble, and a Bottle 105
5-4* Newton, a Table, a Cloth, and a
Glass of Water. 107
5-5* Which Falls Faster, an Object Projected
or Dropped?. 109
5-6* A Small Force Can Beat a Big Force 112
5-7* An Upside-Down Pail of Water That
Does Not Spill. 114
5-8* The Magic Yardstick 117
5-9 The Start-Again Stop-Again Jar 120

List of Suppliers 122

Further Reading 124

Index. 127

*appropriate ideas for science fair project

Introduction

Most of us enjoy a good magic show. This book is filled with projects that appear to be magic, but it is not the magic performed by stage magicians. You will not learn how to hide items in your palm or use trapdoors to make people emerge mysteriously from a trunk. These puzzling tricks are not necessary to have magic happen. Nature provides its own mystery. The "magic" you will do is much easier than the magic performed by magicians on a stage. All you have to do is put the right things together at the right time. Nature will take care of the rest and put on a magic show. Nevertheless, you can use what you learn to entertain friends and family. You might even organize a show and bring both science and entertainment to a number of audiences. You should practice all experiments before performing a show.

In doing these experiments, which will appear to be magic to the people who watch your show, you will learn a lot of science. Each bit of "magic" is based on a scientific principle. You will come to understand why things, which can seem so mysterious to someone who observes your "experiments," are really nothing more than natural events based on scientific principles.

Most of the materials you will need to carry out your projects can be found in your home, a hardware store, or a supermarket. For a few of the experiments, you may want to ask to borrow an item or two from your school's science department. If the school's policy prevents your teachers from letting you take equipment home, you can probably carry out these projects at school during your free time.

For some of the activities, you may need one or more people to help you. It would be best if you work with friends or adults who enjoy science as much as you do. In that way, you will all enjoy what you are doing. **If any project involves the risk of injury, it will be clearly stated in the text. In some cases, to avoid any danger, you will be asked to work with an adult. Please do so.** We do not want you to take any chances that could harm you.

Like a good scientist, you will find it useful to record your ideas, notes, data, and anything you conclude from these projects in a notebook. By so doing, you can keep track of the information you gather and the conclusions you reach. Record keeping will allow you to refer to what you have done, and that may help you in doing other projects.

Science Fairs

If the rules of a particular science fair allow for projects that have a magical flavor, you may be able to adapt some of the material in this book to create an entry. But even if the rules do not allow such projects, some of the "Exploring on Your Own" suggestions that follow experiments with an asterisk (*) can lead to projects that would be appropriate for a science fair.

Bear in mind, however, that judges at science fairs do not reward projects or experiments that are simply copied from a book. Plugging numbers into a formula you do not understand will not impress judges. A graph of data collected from experiments you have done that is used to find a relationship between two variables would be more likely to receive serious consideration.

Science fair judges reward creative thought and imagination. It is difficult to be creative or imaginative unless you are really interested in your project. Consequently, be sure to choose a subject that appeals to you. And before you jump into a project, consider, too, your own talents and the cost of materials you will need.

If you decide to use a project found in this book for a science fair, you should find ways to modify or extend it. This should not be difficult, because you will probably discover that as you do these projects, ideas for new experiments will come to mind. These experiments could make excellent science fair projects, particularly because the ideas are your own and are interesting to you.

If you decide to enter a science fair and have never done so before, you should read some of the books listed in the "Further Reading" section, including *Science Fair Projects—Planning, Presenting, Succeeding*, which is one of the books in this series. These books deal specifically with science fairs. They will provide plenty of helpful hints and useful information that will enable you to avoid the pitfalls that sometimes plague first-time entrants. You will learn how to prepare appealing reports that include charts and graphs, how to set up and display your work, how to present your project, and how to relate to judges and visitors.

Safety First

Most of the projects included in this book are perfectly safe. However, the following safety rules are well worth reading before you start any project.

1. Do any experiments or projects, whether from this book or of your own design, under the supervision of a science teacher or other knowledgeable adult.

2. Read all instructions carefully before proceeding with a project. If you have questions, check with your supervisor before going further.

3. Maintain a serious attitude while conducting experiments. Fooling around can be dangerous to you and to others.

4. Wear approved safety goggles when you are working with a flame or doing anything that might cause injury to your eyes.

5. Do not eat or drink while experimenting.

6. Have a first-aid kit nearby while you are experimenting.

7. Do not put your fingers or any object other than properly designed electrical connectors into electrical outlets.

8. Never experiment with household electricity except under the supervision of a knowledgeable adult.

9. Do not touch a lit high-wattage bulb. Lightbulbs produce light, but they also produce heat.

10. Many substances are poisonous. Do not taste them unless instructed to do so.

11. If a thermometer breaks, inform your adult supervisor. Do not touch either the mercury or the broken glass with your bare hands.

1

There Is Magic in the Air

Throughout this book, the activities are written as if you will be performing your science "magic" before an audience. You may, of course, do some of these experiments in front of friends, relatives, classmates, elementary-school classes, or other audiences. If you do, you will want to rehearse your act before making any public presentations. On the other hand, you may prefer to do these experiments by yourself simply because you can learn more about science in a way that is entertaining. Whatever your approach, enjoy doing the experiments and discover a lot about science.

At the end of each experiment, you will find a section entitled "The Science Behind the Magic," which explains the scientific principles involved in what may appear to be magic. If you do these experiments as scenes for a "Science Through Magic" act, you may or may not choose to share this information with your audience.

The projects in this chapter are all related to the pressure exerted by the air that makes up Earth's atmosphere. Because air has no color or odor and a very low density (about 1.2 grams per liter), we are often unaware of its presence. Despite the fact that air weighs only about 1/1,000 as much as an equal volume of water, it forms a "sea" more than 100 kilometers (60 miles) deep. Since we live at the bottom of this sea of air, the air pushes on every square centimeter of us and everything else on the surface of the earth with a force of about 10 newtons (N). (A newton is a unit used in measuring force; 1.0 N is equal to 0.22 pounds.) The pressure of the air is 10 newtons per square centimeter (N/cm^2) or 14.6 pounds per square inch (lb/in^2).

To get a sense of how large this pressure is, consider the palm of your outstretched hand. It is probably about 7.5 cm (3 in) wide and 7.5 cm long. Its area, therefore, is about 56 cm^2. You would have to hold 560 newtons (125 pounds) in your palm to have a pressure equal to the amount of pressure the atmosphere puts on your hand.

You may wonder then how you can possibly raise your hand as easily as you do. The reason is that the air is pushing upward on your hand (and the rest of your body) with forces that are as large as those pushing downward. Air is made up of tiny molecules, far too small to see, that are all in constant motion. They collide with you and with everything else in contact with air. Like anything that bumps into you, they exert a force on you. Because they are moving in all directions, they exert as much push on the bottom of your hand as they do on the top.

The activities in this chapter will help make you more aware of air and the pressure it exerts on everything it touches.

1-1*
A Balloon in a Bottle

Place a balloon inside a 1-liter soda bottle, as shown in Figure 1a. Leave the mouth of the balloon outside the bottle so you can blow into it. If you do this as part of a science magic show, invite a member of your audience to try to blow up the balloon. The person will find it impossible to do.

Things you will need:

- 2 balloons
- 1/2 or 1-liter (pint or quart) soda bottle
- plastic drinking straw

Remove the balloon and insert a plastic drinking straw into the bottle. Put a new balloon (to avoid transferring any germs from the first balloon) into the bottle. (See Figure 1b.) You can now fill the bottle with the balloon by blowing air into the balloon.

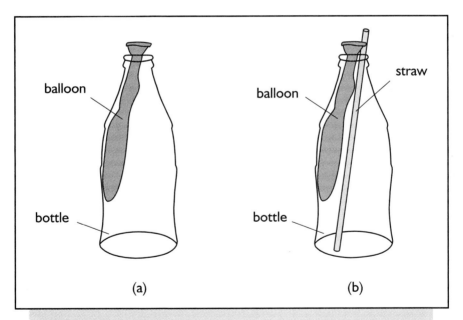

balloon

bottle

(a)

balloon

straw

bottle

(b)

Figure 1. a) It is impossible to blow up the balloon in the bottle. b) Adding a straw makes it possible to blow up the balloon because air can now escape from the bottle as it is compressed by the expanding balloon.

The Science Behind the Magic

The straw allows air to escape from the bottle as it is replaced by the air you blow into the balloon. Without the straw, the balloon quickly seals the mouth of the bottle. As a result, no air can escape. The pressure exerted by the trapped air becomes compressed. Soon the pressure of the trapped air becomes greater than the pressure the person from the audience can exert by blowing into the balloon.

Exploring on Your Own

Design and carry out an experiment to determine how much pressure (above atmospheric pressure) a person can exert by blowing air from his or her lungs. How does it compare with the pressure of the atmosphere at sea level?

How does a barometer measure atmospheric pressure?

1-2
A Funnel That Will Not Empty

If you punch a hole in the side of a water-filled can below the water, water will flow out of the can. The pressure of the air and the column of water above the hole is greater than the pressure of the air alone outside the hole. Water always flows from higher pressure to lower pressure.

Things you will need:

- plastic funnel
- one-hole rubber stopper; hole should match size of funnel's spout
- flask or bottle, about 250 mL (1/2 pint)
- water colored with food coloring
- container to hold water

To begin this bit of science magic, insert the spout of a plastic funnel through the hole of a one-hole rubber stopper. Place the stopper loosely into the neck of a flask or bottle. Hold the rubber stopper so it remains loose in the neck of the flask or bottle as you pour a small amount of colored water from another container into the funnel. Your audience should be able to see the water flowing into the flask or bottle. Empty the water back into its original container.

While you are emptying the water, use your hand, out of sight of the audience, to push the stopper firmly into the mouth of the flask. Now invite someone from the audience to pour the water into the funnel. This time the water remains in the funnel, as shown in Figure 2a. Very little water enters the flask or bottle.

Finally, remove the stopper and funnel from the flask and pour most of the water into the flask. Then insert the stopper with the funnel tightly into the neck of the flask, and turn the apparatus upside down, as shown in Figure 2b. Very little water escapes, most of it remains in the flask.

If someone thinks you have plugged the funnel's spout, turn the apparatus upright and remove the funnel and stopper. Show them that the funnel's spout is open by letting some water flow through

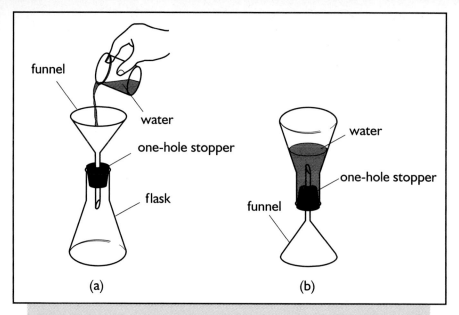

it. Put the stopper firmly into the bottle or flask and turn it upside down again. The water still remains in the flask.

The Science Behind the Magic

When the funnel is above the flask and the stopper is loose, air can escape from the flask as it is replaced by water pouring through the funnel. When the stopper is firmly in the mouth of the flask, air cannot escape. The water that enters the funnel compresses the air below it enough to make the pressure inside the flask equal to the pressure of the air and the small column of water in the funnel. Since pressures are equal, water will not flow through the funnel.

When you turn the funnel and flask upside down, a few drops of water enter the funnel. This increases the volume of air trapped above the water and, thereby, lowers the pressure of the air. Since the pressure of the air beneath the funnel is equal to the pressure of the air and water above, the water remains in the flask. Allow some air into the flask by placing a straw in the funnel, and water will flow out.

16

1-3
A Bottle That Will Not Stop

Submerge a plastic bottle in a pail of water. When the bottle is full of water, screw on its cap and remove it from the pail. Hold the bottle up so the audience can see that it is full and not leaking. Then ask someone from the audience to hold the bottle. When you hand it to the person, water begins to leak from the bottom of the bottle. Take the bottle back and the water immediately stops.

The Science Behind the Magic

The reason the bottle does not leak when it is in your hand is not because you have a magic touch, but because you know *where* to touch. Before the show, use a nail to punch two holes in the bottle—one in the bottom and a second in the side near the top, as shown in Figure 3.

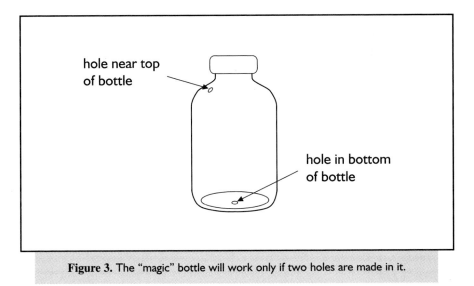

hole near top of bottle

hole in bottom of bottle

Figure 3. The "magic" bottle will work only if two holes are made in it.

17

When you remove the bottle from the pail, put one of your fingers over the hole near the top of the bottle. After a few drops of water fall out of the bottom hole, the bottle stops leaking. After a few drops fall from the bottom hole, the volume of the air trapped above the water increases. This reduces the pressure of the trapped air until it is less than the air pressure outside the bottle. Since the pressure of the air on the outside of the hole is equal to the pressure of the air and water above the hole, the water remains in the bottle. Once you remove your finger, the air above the water is exposed to the outside air, and air pressure forces air into the space at the top of the bottle. The pressure at the bottom of the bottle is now greater than the air pressure outside it, so water will flow from the bottle.

When the top hole is open, can you explain why the pressure at the bottom of the bottle is greater than the air pressure outside the bottle?

1-4*
Getting a Lift with Air Pressure

Things you will need:
- suction cup; buy one about 4.5 cm (1.75 in) in diameter at a hardware store
- card from a deck of playing cards
- an adult
- drill

Remove any hooks or other devices that may be attached to the suction cup. **Ask an adult** to drill a small hole through the center of the cup. Place the cup on a playing card and press down, covering the hole in the cup with your index finger. Then lift the cup and card together from the table. If you want to add a little showmanship to the act, rub the card a few times and say a few magic words before you lift it.

Then invite someone from the audience to lift the card in the same way. It is not likely that they will be able to do so.

The Science Behind the Magic

When you placed the suction cup on the card, you covered the hole in the center of the cup with your index finger and then pressed down. As you pressed down, you squeezed some air from the cup. As you pick up the cup, it begins to spring back to its original shape. As a result, the pressure of the trapped air in the cup is now less than the pressure of the air in the room. Keeping the hole covered with your finger maintains that low pressure. The air pressure below the card is now greater than the pressure of the air in the cup above the card. Consequently, air pressure holds the card against the cup. If you remove your finger, air will enter the cup, the pressure inside the cup will become equal to the air pressure, and the card will fall.

Exploring on Your Own

How does atmospheric pressure change with altitude? You can measure air pressure with an aneroid barometer, which, unlike a mercury barometer, can be carried easily from place to place. Can you detect a difference in air pressure while riding in an elevator? Can you detect a difference in going from one floor of a building to another? Does the barometer indicate pressure changes as you go up and down hills in a car or a bus?

Build a barometer that uses water instead of mercury. How long a tube will you need to measure air pressure with such a barometer?

1-5
Air Pressure Can Be a Real Crusher

Because this activity requires heat and hot objects, do it under adult supervision.

Use soap and warm water to thoroughly wash an empty one-gallon metal can. The washing should remove any small amount of solvent, such as alcohol, that may remain in or on the can. Then pour a cup of water into the can. Leave the opening at the top of the can uncovered. **Ask an adult** to place the can on a hot plate or stove burner. If this is being done before an audience, you can do some other science magic while the water is heating.

Things you will need:

- soap and warm water
- empty 1-gallon metal can
- cup of water
- an adult
- hot plate or stove
- work gloves or pot holder
- heat-proof mat or thick stack of newspapers
- screw-on cap or rubber stopper that fits the opening on the top of the can
- large cloth
- cold water

After the water reaches the boiling point (100°C or 212°F), let it boil for several minutes so that steam replaces most of the air in the can. **Ask the adult to put on work gloves or use a pot holder** to remove the can from the heat. The can should be placed on a heat-proof mat or on a thick stack of newspapers. **The adult** should then immediately screw the cap back on or put a rubber stopper with no holes into the opening on the top of the can.

Cover the can with a large cloth that has been soaked in cold water. Wave your hands and say a few magic words as you wait for air pressure to do its job on the can. From the creaking sounds beneath the cloth, you will know that the can is being crushed. When the noises stop, remove the cloth to reveal the crushed can to the audience.

The Science Behind the Magic

As the water boiled, it produced steam. The steam forced air out the top of the can, so that steam replaced most of the air that had filled the can before. The steam-filled can was closed before the steam, which had replaced the air in the can, could condense. As the steam condensed, the pressure inside the can decreased because there were fewer molecules of steam slamming into the inside walls of the can. Meanwhile, the pressure of the air pushing on the outside of the can remained unchanged. Because the pressure on the outside of the can became much greater than the pressure on the inside, the can collapsed. For example, suppose the pressure inside the can fell to 3 N/cm^2 (4.4 lb/in^2), while the pressure outside remained at 10 N/cm^2 (14.6 lb/in^2). The difference in pressure between the outside and inside of the can would be 7 N/cm^2 or 10.2 lb/in^2. If the can's surface area was 1,500 cm^2 (230 in^2), the total force pushing inward on the can would have been

1,500 cm^2 x 7 N/cm^2 = 10,500 N, or 2,300 pounds (1.15 tons).

The can's collapse is certainly not mysterious when you understand the science behind it.

1-6*
A Geyser

Because this activity requires heat and hot objects, do it under adult supervision.

Air pressure can crush a metal can, as you saw in the previous activity. The same air pressure can be used to fill a vessel with water.

The cold water that you will transfer by air pressure can be placed in a large drinking glass together with a drop or two of food coloring to make the liquid more visible. You will need a Pyrex glass flask (250 mL or larger) and a one-hole rubber stopper that fits the neck of the flask. You will also need a long

piece of glass or rigid plastic tubing that will extend well into the flask and 10–15 cm (4–6 in) beyond its neck (see Figure 4a). Lubricate the surface of the tubing with petroleum jelly, glycerin, or liquid soap so it will slide easily through the hole in the stopper. **Ask the adult to put on gloves and, using a twisting motion, carefully slide the tubing through the hole in the stopper.** He or she should hold the tubing close to the stopper to avoid breaking it. If the tubing does not slide easily, get a length of tubing with a smaller diameter or find a stopper with a larger hole. **The adult should not try to force the tubing. Bad cuts can occur if the tubing breaks!**

With the equipment in place, you are now ready to carry out this part of your show **under adult supervision**. Pour about 30 mL

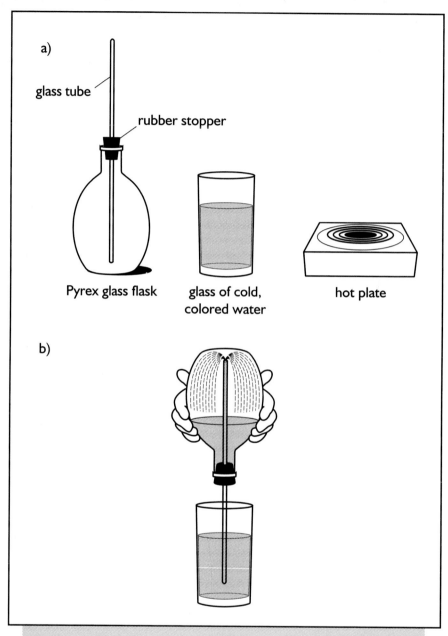

Figure 4. a) You will need a flask, a rubber stopper, a long piece of rigid tubing, a heat source, and a glass of cold water. b) Place the lower end of the glass tube extending from the inverted flask into a glass of cold colored water. As the steam in the flask condenses, a "geyser" will soon emerge from the tube's upper end and fill the flask.

(1 oz) of water into the Pyrex glass flask. Heat the water to boiling on a hot plate or stove burner. Let the water boil for several minutes so that the flask becomes filled with steam. (While the water is being heated, you might do another part of your act.)

After steam has replaced the air in the flask, put on heavy gloves or wear an oven mitt so you can remove the flask from the heat. Place the flask on a heat-proof pad or a thick stack of newspapers. Immediately insert the stopper and tube into the flask, invert it, and hold it so that the lower end of the tube is in the glass of colored water, as shown in Figure 4b. Soon your audience will see a "geyser" as water flows up the tube from the glass and into the flask.

The Science Behind the Magic

As the steam in the flask condenses, the pressure inside the flask decreases. Air pressure forces water from the glass up the tube and into the flask. As soon as the cold water reaches the flask, the remaining steam quickly condenses, causing water to flow rapidly up the tube and into the flask, creating a geyser.

Exploring on Your Own

In the early 1600s, Galileo heard workmen say that a pump could not lift water if the pump was more than 10 m (33 ft) above the water level. Through experiments, Galileo found that the workmen were right. Why can't pumps lift water if they are more than 10 m above the water level?

The water level in deep wells is often more than 30 m (100 ft) below the ground. How is water obtained from such wells?

1-7*
A Ping-Pong Ball That Defies Gravity

Your audience will enjoy it when you place a Ping-Pong ball in the upwardly directed airstream from a vacuum cleaner hose connected to the blower outlet. The ball floats serenely in the airstream, as shown in Figure 5a.

Things you will need:
- Ping-Pong ball
- vacuum cleaner with hose connected to blower outlet
- funnel
- 2 balloons
- string

After you grab the Ping-Pong ball and place it on the floor, they will marvel again as you hold a funnel firmly in the end of the vacuum cleaner hose and lift the ball from the floor. The ball darts about the inside surface of the funnel, as shown in Figure 5b, until you turn off the power leading to the vacuum cleaner. If you have good lung power, you can lift the ball by blowing air into the funnel.

Finally, as a climax to this act, you forcibly blow air between two balloons suspended by strings from a support (Figure 5c), such as a kitchen cabinet. As if driven by some mysterious force, the balloons move together.

The Science Behind the Magic

All the action in this activity is based on Bernoulli's principle. Where the velocity of a fluid (a gas or a liquid) is high, the sideways pressure is low. The Ping-Pong ball in both cases was in a fast-moving airstream. The pressure within that stream was lower than the pressure of the nonmoving air that surrounded it. Consequently, the ball stayed within the fast-moving airstream.

When you blew between the two balloons, the pressure between the balloons became less than the air pressure on the outside of each balloon. As a result, the balloons were forced together.

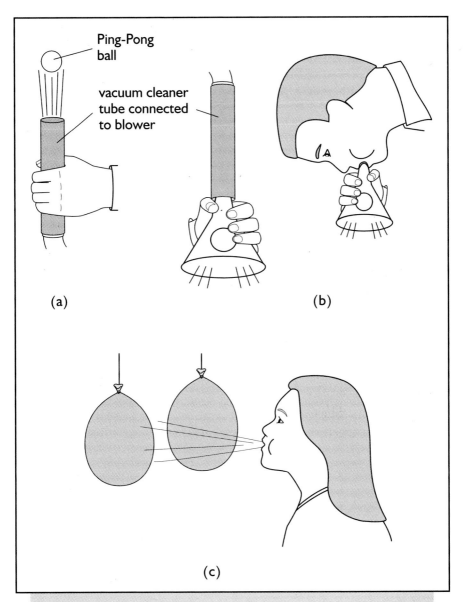

Figure 5. a) A Ping-Pong ball will "float" in an airstream produced by a vacuum cleaner that will blow air. b) The same airstream can be used to lift a Ping-Pong ball with a funnel. If you have good lung power, you can do the same thing by blowing into the funnel. c) What happens when you blow air between two suspended balloons?

Exploring on Your Own

You can make water defy gravity, too. Fill or partially fill a plastic medicine cup or vial with water. Place a card on the cup or vial. Hold the card in place as you turn the cup or vial upside down over a sink (at least until you are confident the water will defy gravity). Remove your hand from the card. The water will remain in the cup or vial.

Of course, gravity cannot be made to disappear and it cannot really be defied. How then can you explain the fact that the water remains in the container?

1-8*
A Voice-Controlled Submarine

Show your audience a model for a submarine. The model consists of an eyedropper partially filled with water in a wide-mouth bottle capped with a rubber stopper or large cork, as shown in Figure 6. You say, "deep dive," and the "submarine" sinks to the bottom of the bottle. You then say "surface," and the vessel rises to the top of the bottle. "Submerge," you shout, and the sub drops to a point between the surface and the bottom.

Things you will need:

- eyedropper
- wide-mouth bottle
- rubber stopper or large cork to fit mouth of bottle
- water

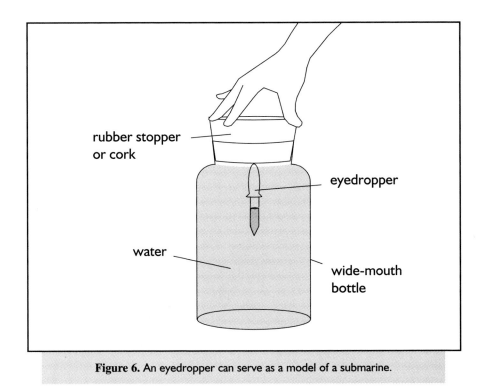

Figure 6. An eyedropper can serve as a model of a submarine.

To prepare your model submarine, nearly fill the bottle with water. Draw enough water into the eyedropper so that it floats in the bottle with just the tip of the rubber bulb above the surface. Place the stopper or cork loosely into the mouth of the bottle. To make the eyedropper fall to the bottom of the bottle, push the stopper farther down into the mouth of the bottle. To make it rise, pull the stopper back up so it just rests in the mouth of the bottle. Pushing the stopper partway into the bottle's mouth will enable you to make the eyedropper sink below the surface, but not to the bottom.

The Science Behind the Magic

When you push down on the stopper, you decrease the space above the water, increasing the air pressure. This increased air pressure is transferred to the water, forcing more liquid into the eyedropper. The rise of water in the eyedropper adds to its weight and causes it to sink. Releasing the pressure by raising the stopper reduces the water in the eyedropper, allowing it to rise. By carefully adjusting the pressure with the stopper, you can give the eyedropper a density equal to that of the water, causing it to float in the middle of the bottle.

Exploring on Your Own

How is the depth of a real submarine controlled?

Build a working model of a submarine.

1-9*
A Mysterious Pair of Balloons

Show your audience a one-hole rubber stopper. To let them know there is a hole in the stopper, run a piece of heavy wire or a stirring rod through the hole. Then blow up a balloon, attach its neck over one end of the stopper,

Things you will need:

- one-hole rubber stopper
- piece of heavy wire or a stirring rod
- 2 identical balloons
- twist-tie

and seal off the balloon with a twist-tie. Attach an uninflated balloon to the other side of the stopper. The two balloons can now be connected through the hole in the stopper once you remove the twist-tie (see Figure 7).

Ask the audience what they think will happen when you remove the twist-tie so air can flow between the two balloons. Most will predict that the air will move from the large balloon into the small one until the two balloons are equal in size.

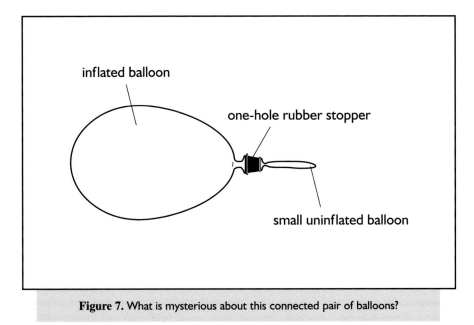

inflated balloon

one-hole rubber stopper

small uninflated balloon

Figure 7. What is mysterious about this connected pair of balloons?

They will be surprised to see that when you open the passage between the two balloons, nothing happens. Air does not flow from the large balloon to the smaller one.

The Science Behind the Magic

Think about how hard it is to force the first few milliliters of air into a balloon. Once you have partially filled the balloon, it is much easier to blow air into it. Since pressure is related to radius, the pressure of the air in a balloon that has a small radius (partially inflated) is greater than the pressure in a balloon with a large diameter (fully inflated). The greater pressure inside the partially inflated balloon makes it harder to blow more air into it.

Exploring on Your Own

Design an experiment to measure the pressure of the air in a balloon. Measure the pressure at various balloon diameters, and then plot a graph of pressure versus balloon diameter. How can you find the approximate volume of the air in a balloon by measuring its diameter? If you release the air in a balloon, will the air occupy more or less space than it did in the balloon?

2

Is Seeing Believing?

The experiments in this chapter have to do with objects and images we see—or think we see. As you will find, the way we see things does not always correspond to the way things really are.

Parts or all of the first five activities in this chapter require that members of the audience have access to simple materials. For an audience of one or two people, this presents no problem. For a larger audience, you can prepare packets of the necessary materials before the show. Or you can run part of the program as a workshop in which members of the audience prepare the materials they will need from a stockpile that you provide.

2-1*
Your Retaining Retina

Put the Fish in Its Bowl

On one side of a white card, draw a picture of a fish. On the other side, draw a fishbowl. Colored marking pens work well. **Ask an adult** to use a fine-tooth saw to cut a narrow slit in the top of a 15-cm (6-in) length of wooden dowel. A vice will hold the dowel steady for cutting. Insert the card into the slot at the top of the dowel. If the card fits loosely, wedge some pieces of paper into the slot to make a tight fit.

Things you will need:

- white card
- fine-tooth saw
- an adult
- colored marking pens
- wooden dowel 15-cm (6-in) long
- vice
- paper
- scissors
- sheet of cardboard
- colored picture
- slide projector and slide
- sheet of white paper
- white stick

When you rotate the dowel between your hands, as shown in Figure 8, the fish will appear to be in the bowl.

Making a Whole from a Part

Use scissors to cut a narrow slit in a sheet of cardboard, as shown in Figure 9. Hold the slit over a picture in bright light. You can see only a small portion of the picture. Now move the cardboard sheet rapidly up and down so the slit scans the entire picture. Even though you can see only a small part of the picture at any one moment, you are able to see the entire picture as long as you keep moving the slit up and down.

A Scene on a Stick

Before the show, you can use a slide projector and a slide to project the slide's image on a distant wall. Then adjust the focus so that the

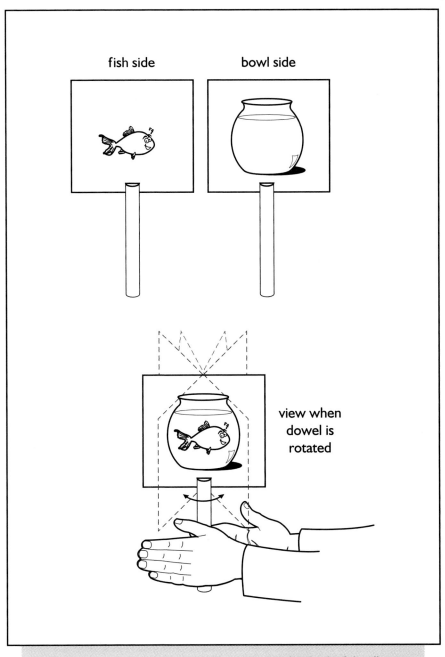

fish side **bowl side**

view when
dowel is
rotated

Figure 8. When you rotate the dowel between your hands, the fish will appear to be in the bowl.

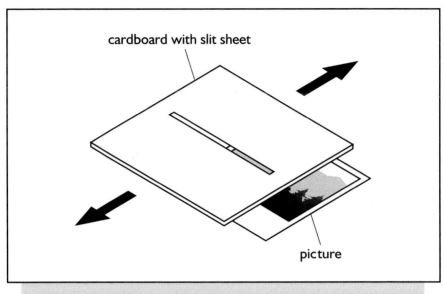

cardboard with slit sheet

picture

Figure 9. A narrow slit is cut in a sheet of cardboard. Move the cardboard up and down rapidly in front of a well-lighted picture. What do you see?

image on the wall is fuzzy but is clear at a point closer to the lens. You can hold a large sheet of white paper several feet in front of the lens and adjust the focus until you get a clear image on the paper.

During your science-through-magic show, turn on the projector. The audience sees a fuzzy image on the distant wall. You tell them you can obtain a clear image by waving a magic wand. Knowing the approximate position where the image is clear, you move a stick that has been painted white rapidly up and down at the position of the focused image. As long as you move the stick quickly, the entire image can be seen on the stick, even though only one part of the image is on the stick at any one moment.

The Science Behind the Magic

These three parts of your show illustrate what is called retinal retention or persistence of vision. The images that form on the retinas at the back of your eyes persist for about 1/15 of a second. It is this persistence of the images that allows you to see the motions in a movie as continuous, even though they are really a series of still pictures. They are flashed on a screen at a rate of 24 or 32 times per second. Since the rate at which the pictures change is faster than the time images remain on your retina, you see the sequence of still pictures as continuous motion.

The same is true of the images you view on a television screen. To make a picture on a television screen, a beam of electrons is swept across every 1/30 of a second. During each sweep, the beam strikes nearly 250,000 tiny phosphor spots that light up when struck by the electrons. Together the spots create an image. Since the images are created so rapidly, motion appears to be continuous.

Exploring on Your Own

Sometimes you will see computer monitors on a television program. Why do the monitors appear to flicker rather than provide a stable image as they do when viewed by themselves?

2-2*
A Letter That Disappears

Prepare a white card for each member of your audience. Near the center of each card use a black felt-tip pen to make a small circle. At a point 5 cm (2 in) to the right of the circle, make a small **x** (see Figure 10). Instruct your audience as follows: "Close your left eye and hold the card at arm's length in front of your right eye. Stare at the circle as you move the card slowly toward your right eye. At some point the **x** will mysteriously disappear. If you move the card closer or farther away, the **x** will reappear."

Things you will need:

- white card for each member of audience

- black felt-tip pen

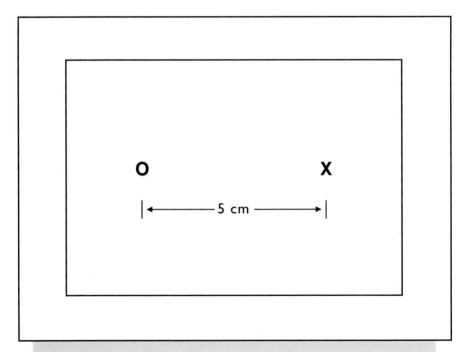

Figure 10. With your left eye closed, the **x** disappears at some point as you move the card back and forth in front of your right eye while staring at the **o**.

The Science Behind the Magic

In the retina, there are light-sensitive cells that respond to light. The nerve impulses that arise in those cells are carried along nerve fibers to the brain by the optic nerve. In the brain, these impulses are combined and give rise to the images we see. Near the center of the retina, there is a small region where the optic nerve enters the back of the eye. There are no light-sensitive cells in that region. As a result, when an image formed by the lens of your eye falls on that small region, no image is formed in the brain because there are no cells responsive to light there. That region is rightly called the blind spot. When the image of the **x** you were looking at falls on the blind spot, you cannot see it.

Exploring on Your Own

Find a way to modify this experiment so that you can make a person disappear from your sight in the same way the **x** disappeared.

2-3
The Lost Coin That Reappears with Water

Tell your audience to form groups of two. Have one person in each pair place a coin on the bottom of an empty teacup or similar opaque container. Have the second person lower his head until the coin just disap-

Things you will need:

• coins

• teacups or similar opaque containers

• water

• containers to hold water

pears below the top edge of the cup, as shown in Figure 11a. Then have the first person slowly pour water into the cup. The coin will become visible again to the person who lowered his or her head. Then have the partners switch places and repeat the activity.

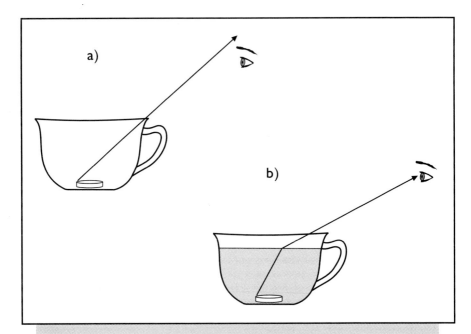

Figure 11. a) Lower your head until a coin in a teacup just disappears from your sight. b) When water is added to the cup, the coin reappears, because light from the coin is now refracted as it leaves the water.

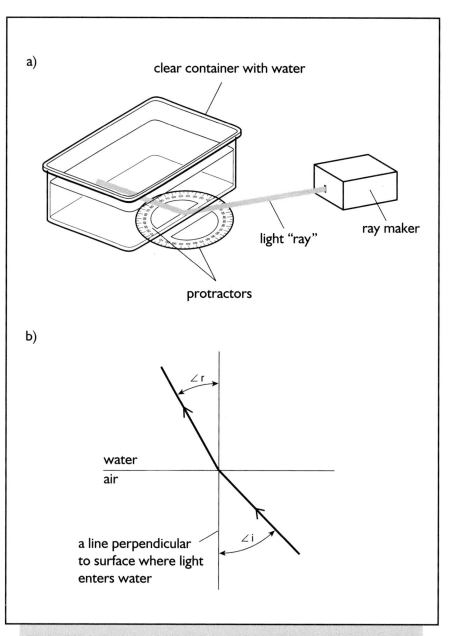

Figure 12. a) The apparatus shown will allow you to measure the angles light makes before and after passing from air to water. b) The drawing shows the angle of incidence (∠ i) of the ray in air and its angle of refraction (∠r) in water.

The Science Behind the Magic

The addition of water causes light from the "hidden" coin to refract (bend) as it passes from water into air. This makes the coin visible again, as shown in Figure 11b.

Exploring on Your Own

Place a pencil in a glass of water. Look at the pencil from the side. Explain why the pencil appears to be broken.

Design a device that will produce a very narrow beam (ray) of light. Use that device together with paper, water, a transparent box with vertical sides, and protractors to measure the angle of the light ray in air and in water, as shown in Figure 12. Do this for a number of different angles and see if you can find a relationship between the angle of incidence ($\angle$ i) and the angle of refraction ($\angle$ r).

2-4*
A Hole in Your Hand

Things you will need:

• sheets of paper

Give each member of your audience a sheet of paper. Ask them to roll the paper into a cylinder about 2 cm (3/4 in) in diameter. Then tell them to look through the tube with their right eye while they focus both eyes on some distant object. Tell them to hold their left hand at arm's length and slowly move it to the right as they continue to focus their eyes on a distant object. They will each see a hole suddenly appear in their left hand.

The Science Behind the Magic

Your eyes are several centimeters apart. As a result, the image formed on the retina at the back of each eye is slightly different. When you look at something close to you, your eyes turn inward toward that object. The two images fall on the central region of each retina. The nerve impulses that go to the brain from the two eyes provide a fused image. The central portion of the image is the same in both eyes. However, the right eye sees farther around the right side of the object and the left eye sees farther around the left side. The fused image produced in your brain provides a three-dimensional view.

When you look at a distant object, both of your eyes are aimed straight ahead. If you take note of a nearby object while your eyes are focused on a distant object, you will see two fuzzy images of that nearby object. Try it! The image of the nearby object falls on the left side of your left retina and on the right side of your right retina. Since these images do not lie on corresponding parts of the two retinas, they give rise to two images that are not fused.

When you placed the paper tube against your right eye, it prevented light from your left hand from reaching your right eye. Instead of seeing two fuzzy images of your hand, you see the fuzzy image of your hand in your left eye superimposed on the image of the distant object in your right eye. The image of the distant object in your left eye is blocked by your outstretched hand. The resulting images are perceived as a distant object seen through a hole in your left hand.

Exploring on Your Own

Investigate the various "clues" that allow you to see the world in three, not two, dimensions.

2-5*
The Mysterious Die

Martin Gardner (no relation to the author) described the following illusion in the December 1991 issue of *The Physics Teacher*. Draw the pattern of three sides of a die on a piece of thin cardboard, as shown in Figure 13a. Cut out the pattern and fold it along the lines, as shown in Figure 13b, to make an *inside-out* die. Tape the die in the back.

Things you will need:
- thin cardboard
- scissors
- black felt-tip pen
- well-lighted room
- table
- tape

Place the die you have made on a table in a well-lighted room. While standing on the other side of the room, look at the die and close one eye. You will soon see the die assume a *right-side-out* appearance. Move a few feet to the right or left. The die will appear to rotate in the opposite direction. Can you explain why?

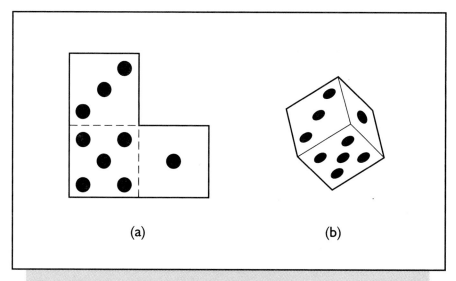

(a)   (b)

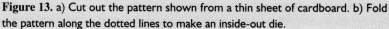

Figure 13. a) Cut out the pattern shown from a thin sheet of cardboard. b) Fold the pattern along the dotted lines to make an inside-out die.

Hold the die on the palm of your outstretched hand. Stare at the far corner of the die with one eye. Now turn your hand slowly in one direction or the other while keeping one eye closed. The die will appear to float as it turns in the opposite direction that your hand turns.

The Science Behind the Magic

By closing one eye, you lose the ability to provide the brain with a three-dimensional view of the inside-out die. (See Experiment 2-4, A Hole in Your Hand.) Your brain is so used to seeing a die as right-side-out that it sees the die in that perspective. By turning your palm to the right with one eye closed, you expose more of the left side of the die. This makes it seem as though the die is rotating to the left.

The floating effect is an illusion. It probably results from the fact that we would expect such a large object to have significant weight. Since it doesn't, we perceive it as virtually weightless. Furthermore, based on experience, we assume the die must be floating if it turns in the opposite direction that the hand turns.

Exploring on Your Own

Can you build a cube without the markings characteristic of a die and obtain the same effects?

2-6
A Suspended Sausage

Tell those in your audience to look at a distant object. Then tell them to continue to focus on the

distant object as they move the tips of their two index fingers together at a point about 15 cm (6 in) in front of their eyes. Next, tell them to move their index fingers slightly apart. They will see a "sausage" apparently suspended in midair.

How far away from your eyes can you hold your index fingers and still see a "sausage?"

The Science Behind the Magic

The explanation is the same as that given for Experiment 2-4, A Hole in Your Hand. You see double images of near objects when your eyes are focused on a distant object.

2-7*
Dragging a Circle

Use clear plastic tape to fasten a sheet of white paper and a sheet of black paper side by side on a piece of cardboard about 40 cm x 27 cm (16 in x 11 in), as shown in Figure 14a. Then use scissors to cut out a gray ring about 2 cm (3/4 in) wide and 20 cm (8 in) in diameter. Glue the ring to the black and white sheets as shown.

Things you will need:
- clear plastic tape
- sheets of white, gray, and black paper
- piece of cardboard about 40 cm x 27 cm (16 in x 11 in)
- scissors
- glue
- ruler or stick

Show the arrangement to your audience. Then ask them to watch closely as you place a stick, such as a ruler, vertically across the gray ring, as shown in Figure 14b. They will suddenly see that the portion of the ring on the white paper appears darker than the portion on the black paper. They will be even more mystified when you move the ruler slowly to the right or left. The darker gray can be "dragged" onto the black side of the sheet and the lighter gray can be pulled onto the white side of the sheet.

The Science Behind the Magic

Your brain interprets brightness in a relative way. A porch light that illuminates your walkway at night may go unnoticed during daylight hours.

When the stick is placed on the gray circle, your eyes immediately respond to the contrast between the gray and white. Small involuntary movements of your eyes cause light from the gray ring to fall on light-sensitive cells on your retina that have been stimulated by the more intense light from the white sheet. (White surfaces reflect more light than gray surfaces do.) The cells stimulated by white light are "tired" and less responsive to light. Therefore, the

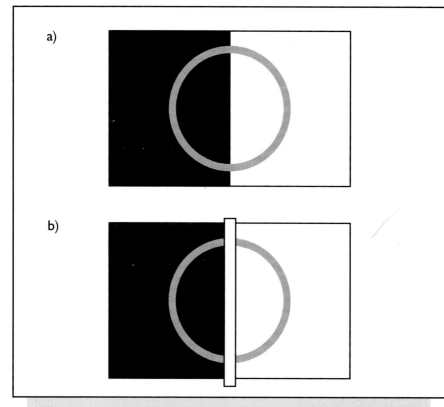

a)

b)

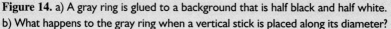

Figure 14. a) A gray ring is glued to a background that is half black and half white. b) What happens to the gray ring when a vertical stick is placed along its diameter?

gray appears darker to your brain than it would if the cells were "fresh" and sent more signals along the optic nerve leading to the brain. For just the opposite reason, the gray on black appears lighter than it would alone.

Exploring on Your Own

Why do you think the lighter and darker portions of the circle can be "dragged" onto the opposite sides of the sheet?

Do you think the two different shades of gray that appear when a stick is laid across the sheet will be evident in a photograph? Try it! What do you find? How can you explain your results?

3

Magic Through Chemistry

The activities in this chapter provide observations that seem magical to those who are not familiar with chemistry. They offer no surprises to chemists.

Most of the chemicals needed to perform chemical "magic" can be found in your kitchen or bathroom. A few of the substances you will need can be purchased at a pharmacy or are probably among your school's supply of science materials. You will have to ask a science teacher if you may use those chemicals.

3-1*
Dancing Raisins

To prepare for this scene you will need to use a small paring knife to cut several raisins into quarters.

With the quartered raisins nearby, nearly fill a glass from a fresh bottle of ginger ale, club soda, or seltzer. Add the raisins and instruct them to dance for your audience.

At first, the raisins will sink to the bottom of the glass. But soon, they rise to the surface, twist and turn about a few times, and then sink back to the bottom of the liquid before they rise again for another dance.

The Science Behind the Magic

Because raisins are denser than the beverage is, they sink when you drop them into the liquid. However, gases are less soluble in water at low pressure than at the higher pressure that existed when the carbonated beverage was bottled. As a result, bubbles of carbon dioxide emerge in fizzy fashion from the solution when the bottle is opened. The bubbles of gas adhere to the raisins. As the bubbles accumulate, the total density of the raisins and adhering gas become less dense than the liquid, and the raisins rise to the surface. There, bumped about by rising bubbles of gas, some of the gas is knocked off the surface of the raisins, and they fall back to the bottom of the glass.

Exploring on Your Own

Design a way to have buttons do a similar dance, using water, baking soda, and vinegar. Explain the source of the bubbles that cause the buttons to dance.

3-2*
Genie in a Bottle

This scene should be prepared immediately before the show. Fill one of two narrow-mouthed bottles to the very top with hot tap water and enough black ink to make the water very dark. The second narrow-mouthed bottle should be filled to the very top with clear, cold tap water.

Things you will need:
- black ink
- 2 narrow-mouthed bottles
- hot and cold water
- paper towel

Tell the audience that a genie resides in the dark-colored bottle and that you are going to try to coax her to emerge. Place a small piece of paper towel on the top of the bottle of clear, cold water before you turn it upside down and place it on top of the bottle with

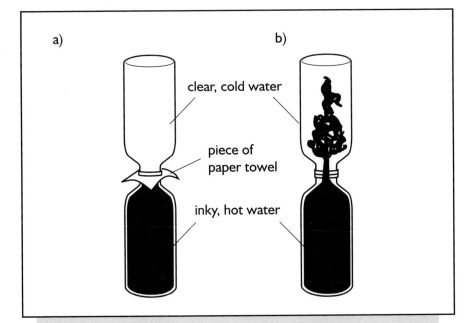

a)

b)

clear, cold water

piece of paper towel

inky, hot water

Figure 15. a) A bottle of cold water is covered with a piece of paper towel. The bottle is then turned upside down and placed on a bottle of hot inky water. b) When the piece of towel is removed, a "genie" emerges from the lower bottle.

the hot, dark liquid, as shown in Figure 15a. The water does not fall out of the inverted bottle because the paper towel, held in place by air pressure, holds the water in the bottle. Air pressure can support a column of water 10 m high as long as there is no air above the column (see Chapter 1).

Carefully pull the piece of towel from between the two bottles as you utter a few words of encouragement to the genie. A "genie" will emerge from the lower bottle and move into the upper bottle, as shown in Figure 15b.

After the show, hold the bottles together as you carry them to a sink where they can be separated.

The Science Behind the Magic

The "genie" is the inky hot water. Because hot water is less dense than cold water, it rises slowly above the cold water as the cold water sinks below the hot water.

Exploring on Your Own

Investigate the relationship between the density of water and its temperature. Is this relationship unique to water?

Investigate what causes the water in lakes and ponds to "turn over" in many parts of the world during late autumn and early spring.

3-3*
Magic Chemical Paper

Warning: Do not put anything containing ammonia near or in your mouth or eyes!

Show your audience a strip of red litmus paper, which you hold over a vial of clear liquid. Then dip the lower half of the paper strip into the liquid for a few seconds and utter a few magic words. When you remove the paper strip, its color has changed. It is now blue!

Immerse the paper strip in a second vial of clear liquid for a few seconds. When you remove the strip, its color has become red again.

The first liquid into which you dipped the strip of red litmus paper was water that contained 3 drops of household ammonia. The second liquid, which caused the color of the paper to change back to red, was water that contained 10 drops of vinegar.

Show your audience another strip of red litmus paper. Dip this strip in a vial of water. Then hold the strip above the mouth of an open bottle of household ammonia. (The bottle's label should be turned away from the audience.) The color of the paper strip changes from red to blue. You then dip the paper strip into the second vial as you did before. The paper's color again changes back to red.

The Science Behind the Magic

Red litmus paper is an acid-base indicator. It is red in acidic substances such as vinegar (a solution of acetic acid), lemon juice, and other fruit juices that contain citric acid. In basic or alkaline substances, such as solutions of ammonia and baking soda (sodium bicarbonate), it is blue. The first vial into which you dip the red litmus paper contains ammonia, a basic solution, so the litmus turns blue. The second vial contains a concentration of acid stronger than the ammonia solution, so the paper turns back to red, indicating an acid.

In the second part of the act, you hold the red litmus strip near the mouth of a bottle of household ammonia. The ammonia vapor dissolves in the wet litmus paper, causing it to turn blue. When you dip the blue litmus paper into the vinegar, the acid solution causes it to turn red again.

Exploring on Your Own

Litmus is a powder obtained from certain species of lichens. Litmus paper is filter paper that has been impregnated with a solution made by dissolving the powdered litmus in water to which a few drops of a weak acid or base have been added. What other natural substances can be used to make acid-base indicators?

3-4
Water to Dragon's Blood to Water

Warning: Do not put anything containing ammonia near or in your mouth or eyes!

Tell your audience you will change water to dragon's blood and then convert it back to water. Remove the cover from what appears to be an empty vial, mutter a few magic words, and proceed to pour a clear liquid into it. The clear liquid suddenly turns deep red. Pour the "dragon's blood" into another apparently empty vial and it suddenly turns clear again.

Things you will need:

- 3 clear vials, plastic cups, or small glasses
- glass or plastic plate to cover one vial, cup, or glass
- phenolphthalein (borrow this liquid indicator from your school's science department)
- eyedropper
- clear vinegar
- ammonia

The clear liquid is water to which you previously added 10 drops of phenolphthalein and 1 drop of clear vinegar. The first "empty" cup actually contains 3 drops of ammonia. (The cover prevents the ammonia from evaporating.) The second "empty" vial contains 10 drops of vinegar.

The Science Behind the Magic

Phenolphthalein is another acid-base indicator. It is clear in an acid and red in a base. The drop of vinegar in the water with the 10 drops of phenolphthalein makes the water slightly acidic. Consequently, the liquid will be clear. When it is added to the vial with 3 drops of ammonia, the ammonia, which is basic, causes the phenolphthalein to turn red, making it appear to be dragon's blood.

The "dragon's blood" is then poured into the second vial, which contains 10 drops of vinegar. There is enough acidic vinegar to neutralize the ammonia and provide an excess of acid. The resulting solution is clear because phenolphthalein is clear in an acid.

3-5
A Bloody Hand

Warning: Do not put anything containing ammonia near or in your mouth or eyes!

Just before this scene begins, spread about 5 drops of phenolphthalein on the palm of your nondominant hand (your left hand, if you are right-handed).

Tell the audience that you have great recuperative powers and can withstand the skin-searing effects of a strong acid. Using an eyedropper, place on your palm a few drops of the liquid you tell them is a "strong acid." (Actually, the liquid is a solution of household ammonia.) Hold up your palm so they can see the "blood." After you wave your hand around in the air for a few seconds, the blood disappears, demonstrating your great recuperative powers. **Wash your hands thoroughly as soon as you finish this scene.**

Things you will need:

- phenolphthalein (borrow this liquid acid-base indicator from your school's science department)
- eyedropper
- household ammonia solution
- small vial or cup to hold the ammonia solution

The Science Behind the Magic

The phenolphthalein on your palm turns red in a base. Since household ammonia solution is basic, your palm turns red when the ammonia is added. It disappears after a short time because the ammonia evaporates.

3-6
Magical Bubbles

Warning: Do not put anything containing ammonia near or in your mouth or eyes!

Before the show, add about 50 mL (1.6 oz) of water, 10 drops of phenolphthalein, a squirt of liquid dish detergent, and 5 drops of household ammonia to a flask or bottle that holds about 250 mL (1 cup). The solution will be red. Place the flask on a thick stack of newspapers to protect any surface beneath the flask.

Things you will need:

- water
- phenolphthalein (borrow this liquid indicator from your school's science department)
- liquid dish detergent
- eyedropper
- household ammonia
- flask or small bottle with a capacity of about 250 mL (1 cup)
- newspapers
- 2 seltzer tablets

Tell your audience that when you add the magic tablets to the flask, the liquid will lose its color and a cascade of bubbles will emerge from the flask. Then drop the seltzer tablets into the flask and the bubbles that form will do the rest.

The Science Behind the Magic

The seltzer tablets contain sodium bicarbonate ($NaHCO_3$) and citric acid ($C_4H_8O_7$). In water, these substances react to form carbon dioxide gas. The citric acid and carbon dioxide, which forms carbonic acid (H_2CO_3) in water, neutralize the ammonia and provide an excess of acid. Since phenolphthalein is clear in acid, the solution quickly loses its red color. Bubbles form and emerge from the flask as the soapy water is filled with carbon dioxide gas.

3-7*
Red, White, and Blue

Warning: Do not put anything containing ammonia near or in your mouth or eyes!

This is a good patriotic act for Flag Day or the Fourth of July. Tell your audience that you are feeling patriotic. As you sing, "Three cheers for the red . . . white . . . and blue!" pour a clear liquid into three clear glasses, plastic cups, or beakers. As you pour into the first cup, while singing "red," the liquid turns red. The liquid poured into the second cup turns white as you sing "white." Similarly, as you sing "blue," the liquid being poured into the third cup turns blue.

Things you will need:

- 3 small glasses, plastic cups, or beakers

(You may be able to borrow the next 3 chemicals from your school's science department)

- phenolphthalein solution
- lead acetate—$Pb(C_2H_3O_2)_2$
- hydrated copper sulfate—$CuSO_4 \cdot 5H_2O$
- household ammonia

Before the performance, line up the three empty cups. Put a few drops of phenolphthalein solution into the first cup. Cover the bottom of the second cup with lead acetate crystals [$Pb(C_2H_3O_2)_2$]. Cover the bottom of the third cup with crystals of hydrated copper sulfate ($CuSO_4 \cdot 5H_2O$). The liquid you pour into the cups is household ammonia.

The Science Behind the Magic

Household ammonia is a solution of ammonia gas dissolved in water. Ammonia (NH_3) reacts with water (H_2O) to form a low concentration of ammonium (NH_4^+) and hydroxide (OH^-) ions.

$$NH_3 + H_2O \rightarrow NH_4^+ + OH^-$$

Ions are atoms or clusters of atoms that carry a charge. The ammonium ion has a charge of $^+1$. The hydroxide ion (OH^-), which is common to bases, has a charge of $^-1$.

In the first cup, the basic ammonia solution causes the phenolphthalein to turn from clear to red. In the second cup, the lead ions (Pb^{++}) in the lead acetate react with the hydroxide ions of the ammonia solution to form lead hydroxide, which is a white solid.

$$Pb^{++} + 2\,OH^- \rightarrow Pb(OH)_2$$

In the third cup, the ammonia reacts with the copper ions in the copper sulfate crystals to form a complex ion of copper and ammonia that has a deep blue color.

$$Cu^{++} + 4NH_3 \rightarrow Cu(NH_3)_4{}^{++}$$

Remember: Do not put any chemicals in your eyes or mouth. Wash your hands thoroughly as soon as you finish the experiment.

Exploring on Your Own

Investigate the compound ammonia (NH_3). How is it made? What are its properties? How is it used commercially?

3-8*
Magic Red to Green to Red

Warning: Do not put anything containing ammonia near or in your mouth or eyes!

To prepare for this scene, add 15 mL (1/2 oz) of *unsweetened* grape juice to 135 mL (4.5 oz) of water in a glass, plastic cup, or beaker. This will reduce the intense red color of the grape juice. Use an eyedropper to add about 5 drops of household ammonia to a second glass. In a third glass, place about 10 drops of vinegar. (You will need to practice to get the right amounts of ammonia and vinegar.)

Things you will need:

- graduated cylinder or measuring cup
- *unsweetened* red grape juice
- water
- 3 glasses, plastic cups, or beakers
- eyedropper
- household ammonia
- clear vinegar

Announce to your audience that you are preparing Ali Baba's magic liquid, which changes magically from red to green. Then utter a few magical words as you pour the grape juice into the second glass. To the amazement of your audience, the juice suddenly turns green.

Then tell them that you can change the green liquid back to red. When you pour the green juice into the third glass, it mysteriously changes back to red.

Remember: Do not drink or taste any liquids used in experiments.

The Science Behind the Magic

Grape juice is an acid-base indicator. It turns green in a basic solution, and ammonia, as you know, is a base. Grape juice is a bluish-purple color in an acid. Consequently, it turns back to its original color when it is poured into the acidic vinegar.

Exploring on Your Own

Do you think unsweetened grape juice is acidic, basic, or neutral? Design an experiment to test your assumption. What do you conclude? **Do not drink the liquid.**

You can prepare an acid-base indicator by placing red cabbage in water and boiling it for a few minutes. After the water cools, pour some into a glass. What is the color of red cabbage juice in an acid? In a base?

3-9*
Iron to Copper

This scene takes a few minutes because the reaction goes slowly. It can be used as an "opener" to which you return after doing several other scenes.

Before starting this bit of chemical magic, you will need to prepare a saturated solution of copper sulfate. You can do this by adding about 50 g (1.75 oz) of the blue crystals of copper sulfate to about 100 mL (3.3 oz) of distilled water, rainwater, or soft water in a glass, plastic cup, or beaker. Stir until most of the blue crystals dissolve. If necessary, add more crystals until no more will dissolve. Any excess copper sulfate can be left on the bottom of the container. You will also need a steel nail a little taller than the container that holds the blue solution of copper sulfate. Use some steel wool to make the nail bright and shiny.

You might begin the scene by announcing that although alchemists never found a way to change lead into gold, you have the magical key needed to change iron into copper. After making your statement, you say a few magic words as you place the steel nail into the copper sulfate solution. Mention that this is slow-acting magic, so you are going to set the vessel aside and return to it later.

When you return to the nail after a few minutes, remove the nail and show your audience that copper has formed on the part of the nail that was immersed in the liquid.

The Science Behind the Magic

When iron (its symbol is Fe) is placed in contact with copper ions (Cu^{++}), which are the positive ions in copper sulfate (the negative

Things you will need:
- about 50 g (1.75 oz) of copper sulfate (buy at hardware store or obtain from school science department)
- distilled water, rainwater, or soft water
- glass, plastic cup, or beaker
- stirring rod or coffee stirrer
- steel nail
- steel wool

ions are the sulfate ions, $SO_4^=$), the iron atoms lose electrons to the copper ions. We say the iron is oxidized by the copper ions. As a result, iron ions (Fe^{++}) dissolve in the solution and copper ions, having gained electrons, are deposited as copper atoms (Cu^0) on the iron nail. The reaction is summarized by the equations below. (A zero above and to the right of the symbol for an atom means the atom has no charge; it has not been ionized.)

$$Fe^0 \rightarrow Fe^{++} + 2 \text{ electrons}$$

$$Cu^{++} + 2 \text{ electrons} \rightarrow Cu^0$$

The net reaction, the sum of the two reactions, is

$$Fe^0 + Cu^{++} \rightarrow Fe^{++} + Cu^0.$$

Exploring on Your Own

Investigate the following questions and write a report: What is alchemy? Who were the alchemists? What did they do? What was the philosopher's stone?

3-10
Disappearing Ink

For this bit of chemical magic, you will need some household bleach (sodium hypochlorite [NaOCl]). **Be sure to keep the liquid bleach away from your eyes, mouth, and skin! After the show, be sure to thoroughly wash the container in which you placed the bleach.**

Things you will need:
• glass, beaker, or plastic cup
• water
• eyedropper
• black ink
• stirring rod or coffee stirrer
• liquid household bleach
• container to hold bleach

Begin this scene by holding a glass, beaker, or plastic cup partially filled with water so your audience can see it. Then add a drop or two of black ink to the water and stir to make the liquid dark. Next, pour a predetermined amount of a clear "magic" liquid (actually bleach) into the dark liquid and stir some more. After some stirring and some words of wizardry, the liquid turns clear.

You will need to practice this act a few times to determine the exact volume of bleach you need to discolor the inky water.

The Science Behind the Magic

Bleach releases oxygen. The oxygen combines with the colored pigments in the ink to produce colorless compounds.

3-11*
Turning Aladdin's Lamp Oil into Ink

To prepare for this act, add about 1/4 teaspoon of cornstarch or flour to an empty glass, beaker, or plastic cup. In an identical container about 2/3 full of water, add about 1/4 teaspoon of tincture of iodine and stir to form a straw-colored liquid. **Iodine is poisonous, so keep it away from your eyes and mouth. Be sure to wash the glasses and spoon thoroughly with soap and water after the show!**

Things you will need:

- teaspoon
- cornstarch or flour
- 2 glasses, beakers, or plastic cups
- water
- tincture of iodine

As the scene begins, point to the straw-colored liquid and tell your audience that you are going to change Aladdin's lamp oil to ink. Then pour the straw-colored liquid into the vessel that holds the "magic powder" (cornstarch). After you pour the liquid back and forth from one container to the other several times, the liquid will turn dark blue.

The Science Behind the Magic

Starch and iodine combine to form a dark blue compound. In fact, the formation of a dark blue color when iodine is added serves as a test for starch. Similarly, if a dark blue color appears when starch is added to an unknown liquid, that liquid must contain iodine.

Exploring on Your Own

Under adult supervision, do some research to find out how iodine can be used to test for the starch found in foods such as potatoes and bread. Then use your knowledge to test for the presence of starch in a variety of foods.

3-12*
Written Secrets

One or all of the scenes in this act can be used to reveal to an audience invisible messages left by a "spirit," "witch," or other medium of your choice.

A Hard-Pressed Message (for a small audience)

A mechanical form of invisible writing can be prepared in a way similar to that used to place watermarks on writing paper. Dip a piece of paper in water. Put the wet paper on a hard surface, such as a kitchen counter. Place a piece of dry paper on the wet paper. Using a ballpoint pen, press down hard as you write a message. It could be a warm greeting, such as a smiley face or WELCOME TO THE SHOW; it could also be a foreboding message, such as BEWARE OF MAGIC-MAKING SCIENTISTS!

Things you will need:

- pieces of paper (10 cm x 10 cm [2.5 in x 2.5 in])
- water
- hard surface, such as a kitchen counter
- ballpoint pen
- stove or hot plate
- an adult
- pan
- lemon juice
- toothpicks
- sugar
- teaspoon
- warm water
- kitchen clamps
- pail of water
- cobalt chloride ($CoCl_2 \cdot 6H_2O$) (ask to borrow from school science department)
- graduated cylinder or measuring cup
- small artist's brush
- medicine cup

Set the wet paper aside to dry. When it has dried, the writing will not be apparent. Dip the paper in water and hold it up to the light. The letters or marks that make up the message will transmit light better than the rest of the paper. Consequently, the message will be quite visible as you look through it, facing a bright window or light.

If you like, this could be used as an opening scene. Each person in the audience could be given one hard-pressed message. They could then dip the paper in a pail of water and hold it up to the light.

Chemical Messages

Because these activities require a stove or hot plate and the possibility of flames, they should be done under adult supervision. Keep a pan of water nearby. Should a piece of paper begin to burn, put it in the water.

A commonly used invisible ink is lemon juice. Use the wide end of a toothpick dipped in lemon juice to write a message on a small piece of paper. Keep dipping the toothpick into the lemon juice as you write. There should be a continuous film of lemon juice along each letter you write. After you have finished writing the message, set the paper aside and let the "ink" dry.

While the lemon juice is drying, write another message on another small piece of paper, using saliva (something you always have with you) as the ink and another toothpick as your pen.

Write still a third invisible message, using a toothpick and a saturated solution of sugar. Add a teaspoonful of sugar to a medicine cup. Nearly fill the cup with warm water and stir with the toothpick you will use to write the message.

When the "ink" on all your messages has dried, you will be ready to reveal the hidden messages. **Under adult supervision,** use a pair of kitchen clamps to hold each piece of paper, in turn, over a stove burner or hot plate, as shown in Figure 16. Hold the paper well above the hot surface so that the paper does not burn. **A pail of water should be beside the stove in case the paper does begin to burn.**

Slowly, the message written in invisible ink on each piece of paper will appear, and you can then show it to your audience.

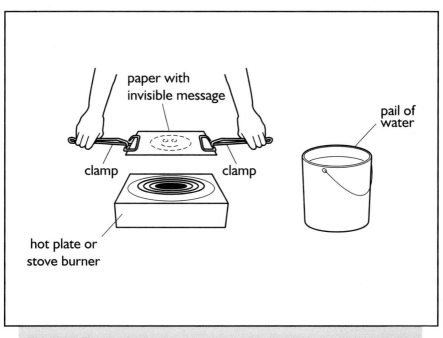

Figure 16. The secret message written in invisible ink can be revealed if the paper on which the message is written is carefully heated.

A Chemical Message in Blue

To write this invisible message, you will need to prepare a solution of cobalt chloride ($CoCl_2 \cdot 6H_2O$). Dissolve as much cobalt chloride as possible in 25 mL (1 oz) of water. This saturated solution will serve as your ink. Use a small artist's brush to write a message on a small piece of paper.

When the water in the solution has evaporated, the tiny, nearly invisible pink crystals of cobalt chloride will remain. **Under adult supervision,** use a pair of kitchen clamps to hold the paper over a stove burner or hot plate, as shown in Figure 16. Hold the paper well above the hot surface so that the paper does not burn. **Keep a pail of water beside the stove in case the paper does begin to burn.**

The message you wrote on the paper will appear in blue "ink."

The Science Behind the Magic

When you wrote the hard-pressed message, you squeezed and flattened the wood fibers in the paper. This made the paper thinner where it had been pressed. As a result, it transmitted more light than the thicker paper surrounding it.

The "inks" used in the chemical messages all contained organic compounds (compounds that contain carbon). When these organic substances were heated, they decomposed, leaving primarily carbon, which is a black element.

The chemical message in blue appears because the water in the hydrated *pink* crystals was removed when the paper was heated. What remains on the paper are the clearly visible *blue* crystals of anhydrous (without water) cobalt chloride ($CoCl_2$).

With time, the blue crystals will react with moisture in the air and re-form pink hydrated crystals.

Exploring on Your Own

Sodium chloride (NaCl), which is ordinary table salt, is not an organic compound. It has no carbon. Consequently, heating dried salt will not produce a visible message written in carbon. See if you can find another way to use salt as an invisible ink.

Develop invisible inks of your own and use them to write secret messages.

3-13*
A Flame That Jumps

Because you will be using matches and working with a burning candle, do this trick under adult supervision.

Light a candle and let it burn for several minutes. Then blow out the candle. You will notice that a stream of light-colored smoke continues to rise from the wick. If you bring a lighted match to that stream of smoke several centimeters above the wick, the flame will follow the smoke stream downward and reignite the wick.

Things you will need:
- candle
- candle holder
- lamp chimney, or glass or plastic cylinder
- an adult
- matches
- wood blocks

For an audience, this trick is best done with a clear lamp chimney or a glass or plastic cylinder over the candle, as shown in Figure 17. The top of the cylinder should be about 10 cm (4 in) above the wick to make the distance that the flame jumps more dramatic. The bottom should be placed on wood blocks.

When you begin the scene, the candle is burning. You announce that you will blow out the candle and relight it without bringing a match to the wick. You then light a match, blow out the candle, and bring the match to the top of the chimney where it can ignite the smoke streaming from the wick. The flame will follow the smoke back to the wick. You can repeat this several times, but the candle must burn long enough so that there will be good stream of wax vapor after the flame is blown out.

The Science Behind the Magic

When you light a candle, the wick burns and melts some of the wax at the top of the candle. The liquid wax moves up the wick by capillary action. As the wax reaches the flame, it changes to a gas and burns.

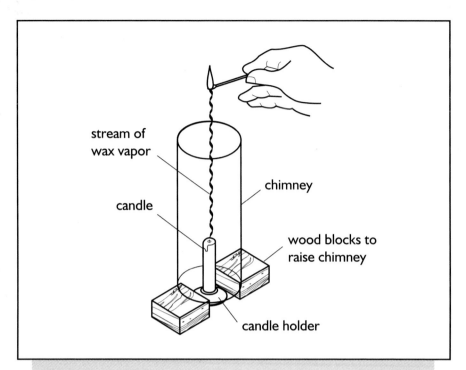

Figure 17. A stream of wax vapor rising from a just-extinguished candle is flammable. If ignited, the flame will follow the vapor trail back to the wick and relight the candle. Blocks are placed under the chimney so that air can flow under it and provide a good source of oxygen for the burning candle.

When you blow out a candle, a stream of flammable wax vapor rises from the wick. Bringing a match to the vapor ignites it, and the flame follows the vapor trail down to its origin. Once the wick cools and fails to emit any more vapor, you cannot reignite it from afar.

Exploring on Your Own

What is capillary action? Investigate how it works.

3-14
A Blue Bottle

Things you will need:

- an adult
- safety glasses
- 500 mL glass flask, preferably round with a flat base
- rubber stopper that fits flask
- 400 mL of water
- balance and weighing papers
- potassium hydroxide (KOH) (ask to borrow from school science department)
- methylene blue (ask to borrow from school science department)
- spatula or spoon to transfer chemicals
- dextrose (glucose) (ask to borrow from school science department or buy from pharmacy)

Because toxic chemicals are used in this activity, prepare the solution under adult supervision. Wear safety glasses while working with these chemicals.

If you can obtain the necessary chemicals and glass flask from your school's science department, this scene could provide a dramatic start and conclusion to your science-through-magic program.

Pointing to a glass flask that holds a cloudy liquid, you say, "That's strange; this liquid used to be blue." You then shake the flask, keeping your hand firmly over the rubber stopper in its neck. The fluid in the bottle suddenly turns blue.

The blue color will slowly fade with time. It will return each time you shake it. If you start your program with this scene, you can return to it periodically throughout the show and conclude with it.

The solution is prepared by adding approximately 2.0 grams (0.07 oz) of potassium hydroxide (KOH) to about 400 mL of water. **(Potassium hydroxide is a poisonous solid similar to lye. Keep it away from your skin, eyes, and mouth.)** Use a spatula or spoon to transfer the potassium hydroxide from its bottle to a weighing paper on the balance. Once weighed, the solid can be poured from the paper into the flask.

Heat will be produced when this strong base is added to water. After the solution cools, add 1.2 grams (0.04 oz) of dextrose (glucose) and a pinch of methylene blue and stir to dissolve the two solids.

The solution is not stable, so you should prepare a fresh solution before each show.

The Science Behind the Magic

In a basic solution, methylene blue turns to a cloudy gray compound. However, when the solution is mixed with oxygen in the air, the cloudy compound is oxidized back to methylene blue, so the solution becomes blue again. In fact, if you look closely, you will see that the surface of the cloudy gray compound, which is in contact with air, remains blue.

4

Magic Through Light and Through "Sticky" Water

The activities in this chapter provide observations that seem magical to those who are not familiar with the physics of light and water. People who have studied physics are less likely to be surprised.

Most of the materials needed to perform the "magic" in this chapter can be found in your kitchen, bathroom, or desk.

4-1*
An Inverted Scene

Hold a water-filled spherical (round) flask or bowl near a white wall or screen, as shown in Figure 18. Invite your audience to view on the wall an inverted miniature image of the scene they can see through a window on the far side of the room. If your program is held at night, you can substitute a clear bright lightbulb for the window.

Things you will need:

- water
- spherical flask or bowl
- white wall or screen
- window with a view or clear, bright lightbulb
- large-diameter convex lens, such as a large magnifying glass

Repeat the procedure, using a large-diameter convex lens in place of the flask or bowl. The lens will provide an even sharper but still inverted image of the scene.

The Science Behind the Magic

The inverted image of the scene or bulb is the result of light from the scene's being refracted by the lens or sphere. The image is the result of the convergence (bringing together) of light rays from the distant object. There is a one-to-one correspondence between the points of light on the distant object (window scene or bulb) that emitted the light and the same points on the image seen on the wall. Such an image—one that can be captured on a screen or wall—is called a real image. It is really there. The images you see in a plane mirror are called virtual images. They only appear to be where you see them (behind the mirror). You cannot capture them on a screen.

For a distant object, the image made when some of its light passes through a convex lens will be very close to the focal point of the lens. (The focal point of a convex lens is the point where parallel rays of light are brought together. See Figure 19a.) This is a convenient way to find the focal point of a lens. If the object is

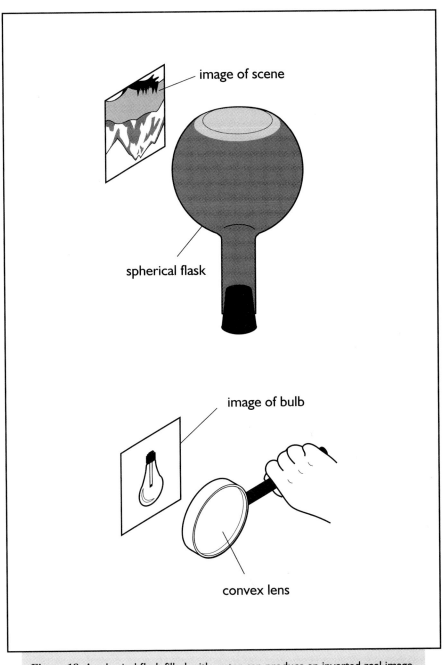

image of scene

spherical flask

image of bulb

convex lens

Figure 18. A spherical flask filled with water can produce an inverted real image. The same can be accomplished with a convex lens.

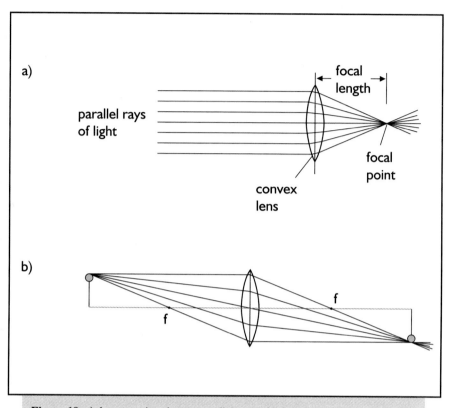

a)

focal
length

parallel rays
of light

focal
point

convex
lens

b)

f

f

Figure 19. a) A convex lens brings parallel rays of light together at a point called the focal point. The distance from the center of the lens to the focal point is called the focal length of the lens. b) If an object is more than a focal length, f, from a convex lens, its image will be real, inverted, and located beyond the focal point on the opposite side of the lens. A real image is one you can "capture" on a screen.

closer to the lens (but more than a focal length away), the image will be more than a focal length from the lens, as shown in Figure 19b.

Exploring on Your Own

Determine the focal length, f, of a convex lens. Then measure the position and size of an object and its image when the object is at various distances beyond the focal length in front of the lens. You might place the object at distances such as 1/4 f, 1/2 f, f, 2 f, 3 f,

4 f . . . beyond the focal point. Then measure the position of the image in fractions or multiples of the focal length from the focal point on the other side of the lens. How are the products of the positions of object and corresponding image related to the focal length of the lens?

Investigate the image that forms when an object is less than one focal length from a convex lens. Where is it located? What kind of an image is it?

Investigate the images formed by concave lenses. Are they real or virtual? Does a concave lens have a focal length?

4-2*
Upside-Down Shadow

Wrap a tiny piece of masking tape around the sharp end of a pin that has a small, round head, as shown in Figure 20a. The tape will prevent the pin from scratching your eye. Grasp the pin by the tape and hold it close to one eye, as shown in Figure

Things you will need:

- masking tape
- pin with a small, round head
- file card with a pinhole in its center
- bright source of light

20b. Look toward a bright source of light, such as a window or light-bulb. With the pin upright in front of and close to your eye, hold a file card with a pinhole in its center between the pin and the light so that only light coming through the pinhole reaches your eye. You will notice that the shadow of the pin cast on your eye's retina is upside down. When you move the card to one side, the inverted shadow disappears. You now see a very fuzzy upright image of the pin.

If you do this as a scene in your science-through-magic program, provide each member of the audience with a file card and a pin that has its end covered with masking tape. Then they can see the same mysterious inverted shadow that you have seen.

The Science Behind the Magic

The pinhole restricts the amount of light reaching the pin. As a result, only the light between the two rays shown in Figure 20c reach the pin. The pin blocks this light so that an upright shadow of the pin falls on the retina. However, the brain interprets inverted images as being upright, because normally the images on the retina are upside down. The lens in your eye forms an inverted image of the objects you see. (See Figure 20d and Experiment 4-1.) Because your brain has learned to interpret inverted images as right side up, you see an upside-down shadow of the pin.

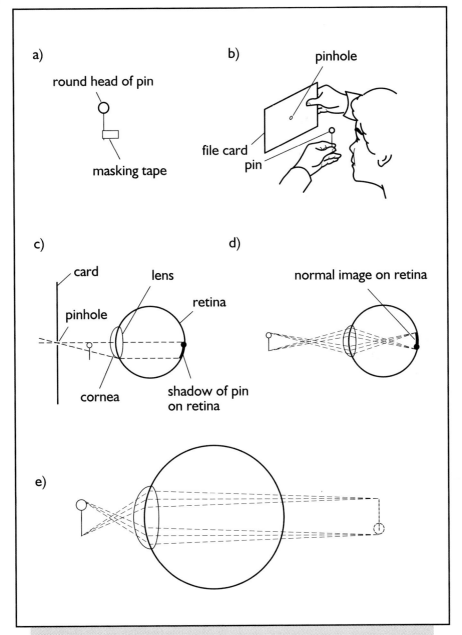

Figure 20. a) A pin should have its sharp end covered with tape. b) Hold the pin close to one eye as you look through a pinhole toward a good source of light. c) Light coming through the pinhole will cast a shadow of the pin on your retina. d) Normally, the images that form on the retinas of our eyes are inverted. e) If an object is very close to your eye, the eye's lens cannot focus the image on the retina. Consequently, the image is fuzzy.

Normally, many light rays from all points on an object reach our eyes. If the object is close to the eye, as was the pin, the lens cannot bend the light enough to form a clear image. As a result, a fuzzy inverted image forms on the retina, as shown in Figure 20e.

Exploring on Your Own

Hold the pin close to your eye and the pinhole only slightly farther away. Now slowly move the card farther from your eye. What happens to the apparent size of the pin's shadow on your retina? Try to explain what you observe.

Investigate pinhole images and how they are made. Are pinhole images always inverted?

Make a pinhole camera and use it to take photographs.

4-3*
Turning Words About

Invite your audience to look through some clear vials or test tubes filled with colored water, as shown in Figure 21a. The words—CAT, FOG, GIRL—written on small white cards and seen through the vials with blue water appear to be upside down, but the words on the cards seen through the vials that hold red

water—OXIDE, CHOICE, BOX—are right side up. You raise the question: How does blue water turn words upside down while red water does not?

In preparing the words for viewing, use some clay to hold the water-filled vials or tubes in place. You can also use the clay to raise the tubes slightly, if necessary, to make the inverted images seen through the water as clear as possible.

The Science Behind the Magic

The vials or tubes are cylindrical lenses. Such lenses focus light along a line rather than to a point. Cylindrical lenses, like convex lenses, can refract (bend) light to produce real inverted images, as shown in Figure 21b.

Of course, the images are inverted regardless of the color of the water in the lens. Someone in your audience may notice that the words OXIDE, CHOICE, and BOX are the same whether right side up or upside down.

Exploring on Your Own

Remember: Never look directly at the sun. It will damage your eyes. If you hold a cylindrical lens in sunlight and place a piece of

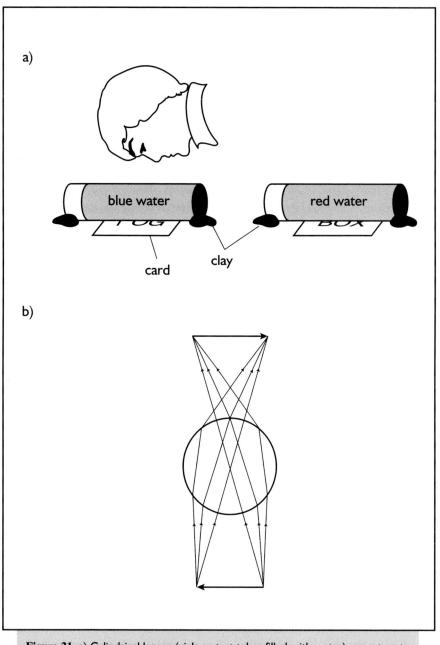

Figure 21. a) Cylindrical lenses (vials or test tubes filled with water) are set up to view words printed on white cards. b) A side view shows how light rays are bent (refracted) when they pass through a cylindrical lens.

white cardboard behind it, what can you expect to see on the screen? Try it! Were you right? If you turn the cylinder 90 degrees, what do you think will happen to what you see on the screen? Try it! Were you right?

You have seen that a cylindrical lens can be used to invert letters. A convex lens can turn letters right for left as well as invert them. Can a cylindrical lens be used to turn letters right for left?

4-4*
Disappearing Glass

Tell your audience that you have found a way to make glass disappear. Place a Pyrex beaker inside one slightly larger in size. If there is printed material on the beakers, turn them so the print has minimal visibility from the audience. Then pour vegetable oil slowly into the smaller beaker. After the smaller beaker

Things you will need:

- 2 Pyrex glass beakers, 1 larger than the other (250 and 400 mL work well); your school's science department probably has Pyrex beakers

- Wesson vegetable oil; this brand seems to give best results, but others may be satisfactory

is filled, the oil spills over into the larger beaker. As the oil rises up

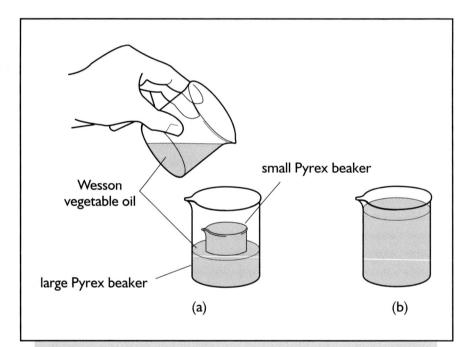

Figure 22. a) Pour Wesson vegetable oil into the smaller of two Pyrex beakers. As the oil spills over into the larger beaker, the smaller beaker slowly disappears. b) When the smaller beaker is submerged in oil, it disappears completely.

the outside of the smaller beaker, it slowly disappears, as shown in Figure 22. Finally, when it is completely immersed in the oil, it disappears entirely.

The Science Behind the Magic

Objects are visible because they reflect light or refract (bend) light. If two clear objects refract light by the same amount, they are the same material as far as light is concerned. Light passing from one such object to another will not be refracted or reflected.

Wesson vegetable oil refracts light in almost exactly the same way as Pyrex glass. Consequently, light is refracted or reflected very little as it passes from Wesson vegetable oil to Pyrex glass or vice versa. As a result, a Pyrex beaker immersed in the oil is virtually invisible.

Exploring on Your Own

What is meant by the index of refraction of a material? How can a substance's index of refraction be determined?

Design and carry out an experiment to find out whether the index of refraction is related to the density of transparent substances.

4-5*
The Magic Mirror

Invite members of your audience, one by one, to look down into a box resting on a table that holds a "magic mirror." As they look into the mirror, they will see an upside-down image of their faces.

Things you will need:

- 2 mirrors, 10–30 cm (4–12 in) on a side
- box into which mirrors will fit snugly
- table
- newspapers to adjust the angle of the mirrors

After they have all looked into the box, turn the box 90 degrees, and invite them to look into the box once more. This time, tell them to wink at their own image. They will be surprised to see that, unlike a normal image, this image winks back with the same eye they wink. If they wink their right eye, their image winks its right eye. As you know, normally, when you wink your right eye, your mirror image winks its left eye.

In preparing the mirrors, place them in the box so that they are at right angles and form a V, as shown in Figure 23a. Use crumpled newspapers to adjust the angle of the mirrors. You can best determine when the mirrors are at a right angle (90°) by looking into them as you adjust the angle between them. The images near the line where the mirrors meet should fuse to form a single upside-down image of your face. When they do, the mirrors are at a right angle.

After you turn the box 90 degrees, you can again adjust the mirrors, if necessary, by finding the positions that produce a single image of your face. When you look at your image formed by these two mirrors, you will see that your image winks the same eye that you do.

The Science Behind the Magic

Figure 23b shows that two mirrors at right angles form three images. The two images on the sides, I_1 and I_2, are the result of light

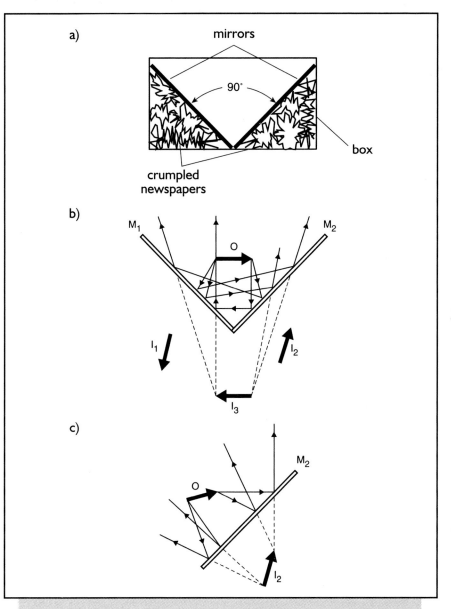

Figure 23. a) View through side of box that holds two mirrors at right angles. b) Two mirrors M_1 and M_2 are at right angles (90°). An object, O, is between (or near) the two mirrors. As expected, virtual images I_1 and I_2 can be seen behind mirrors M_1 and M_2. However, a third image, I_3, can be seen. I_3 is the result of light rays that are reflected twice. Only four of the light rays that give rise to I_3 are shown. As you can see, I_3 is reversed in terms of the way we normally see a mirror image. c) Images I_1 and I_2 are formed by ordinary single reflection of rays. In the diagram, four rays are used to show how image I_2 is formed in M_2. I_1 is formed in a similar manner in M_1.

rays reflected from a single mirror. They are formed by ordinary reflections from a plane mirror, as shown in Figure 23c. The center image, I_3, is formed by light that has been reflected twice, once by each mirror. Since it has been reflected twice, it is an image of an image. As a result, right for left has become right for right.

As you can see, the image of the arrow, which could represent the top and bottom of a person's face, is seen as being upside down. If the arrow represented the left and right sides of a person's face, the object's left eye would be the image's left eye.

Exploring on Your Own

Investigate the formation of images in plane mirrors. How can you find the apparent position of an image in a plane mirror? How can you find the position of an image in a concave mirror? In a convex mirror?

With two mirrors at 90 degrees to each other, you see three images. How many images do you see when the mirrors are at 60 degrees? At 45 degrees? At 30 degrees? At other angles? Can you find a relationship between the number of images and the angle between the mirrors?

4-6*
Floating Steel

Show your audience a large steel paper clip. Drop the paper clip into a glass of water. To no one's surprise, the paper clip sinks in the water. Now put another identical paper clip on a dining fork. Using the fork, gently place the paper clip on the surface of some water in a large plastic

container, as shown in Figure 24. (The plastic container must be very clean and thoroughly rinsed.) Amazingly, the paper clip floats on the water! If your audience looks closely, they can see the indentations that the steel makes on the water's surface.

Then announce that you have a magic fluid that will make the paper clip sink without your touching it. Place a drop of liquid on the water and the paper clip sinks.

The Science Behind the Magic

Steel is more dense than water, so it sinks in the liquid. However, water molecules are strongly attracted to one another. At the surface of water, the strong inward pull on the surface molecules creates a skinlike effect (called surface tension) that enables the water to support a paper clip, a pin, or similar small pieces of metal. It is the same "skin" that allows insects to walk on water.

The drop of magic liquid is really liquid detergent or soap. The soap molecules get between the water molecules and thereby reduce the forces that hold the water molecules together. Without a "skin," the water surface is unable to support the paper clip, and it falls to the bottom of the container.

The surface tension of water is easily reduced by foreign substances. Therefore, you must be sure that the container holding

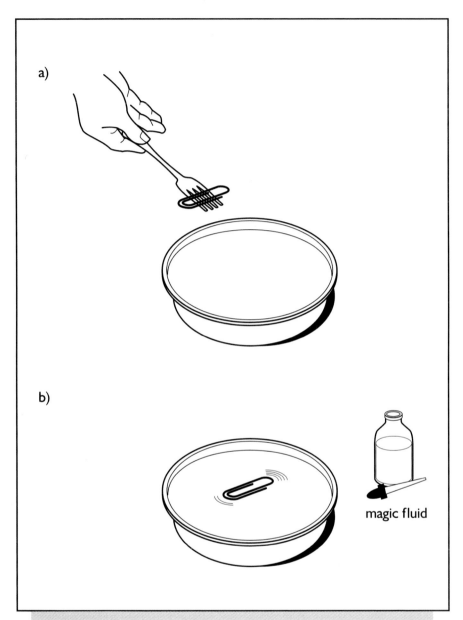

a)

b)

magic fluid

Figure 24. a) Using a dining fork, you can gently place a steel paper clip on the surface of some water. b) The water will support the paper clip so that it floats on the surface of the water. What happens when a drop of "magic" fluid is added to the water?

the water has been thoroughly washed and rinsed. Any soap remaining on the dish could reduce the surface tension of the water. With less surface tension, the water would be unable to support the paper clip.

Exploring on Your Own

How does the surface tension of water compare with the surface tension of other liquids such as alcohol, vinegar, and cooking oil? Design and conduct experiments to find out. How can the surface tension of a liquid be measured?

4-7
Water on a String

Tell your audience that you can make water defy gravity. Then tie one end of a wet string to the top of the handle of a large measuring cup or pitcher with a narrow spout filled with colored water. While you tip the cup or pitcher up slowly with one hand, as shown in Figure 25, use your other hand to hold the free end of the string. The string should

Things you will need:

- water
- string
- large measuring cup or pitcher with a narrow spout
- empty container
- food coloring
- long piece of glass rod or tubing (optional)
- pencil (optional)

be held tautly against the spout of the cup or pitcher and extend to a point above an empty container some distance away. Pour very slowly and the colored water will flow along the string and collect in the container below your hand.

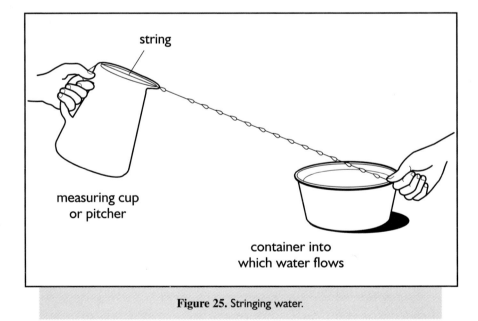

string

measuring cup
or pitcher

container into
which water flows

Figure 25. Stringing water.

The Science Behind the Magic

Water adheres to the string and, as you saw in the previous experiment, water itself is cohesive. The forces within the water and between the water and the string are stronger than the forces of gravity acting on the water. Consequently, the water will flow along the string from the cup or pitcher to the container at the end of the string, where it collects.

If you would like, you can also show that water will flow along a wet piece of glass or a pencil.

4-8*
An Underwater Bulb

Use two insulated wires to connect a flashlight bulb in a bulb holder (socket) to a 6-volt lantern battery, as shown in Figure 26. Ask your audience what they think will happen if you lower the bulb into a beaker or glass filled with water. Most people think a lightbulb will go out if placed in water. They will probably be surprised to see that the bulb continues to glow brightly underwater.

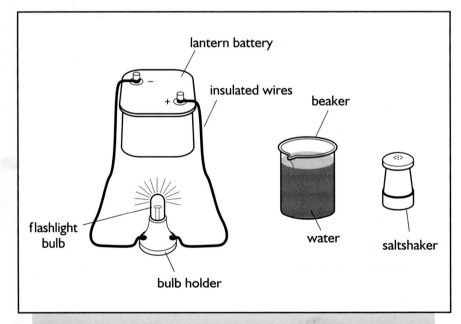

Things you will need:

- 2 long insulated wires
- flashlight bulb and bulb holder
- lantern battery
- beaker or glass
- water
- salt and saltshaker

Next, ask them what they think will happen if salt is added to the water. Some may think the salt will cause the bulb to "short out."

Figure 26. What will happen to a glowing flashlight bulb if it is immersed in water? In saltwater?

96

Invite someone to sprinkle salt from a saltshaker into the water. The bulb still glows brightly even when immersed in saltwater.

The Science Behind the Magic

The metal wires leading to the bulb and the wire filaments inside the bulb are much better conductors of electricity than either water or saltwater. Consequently, very little electric charge flows through the liquid.

Exploring on Your Own

You may have noticed some small bubbles forming at the connections to the bulb holder when the bulb and its holder were immersed in saltwater. What were those bubbles and why did they form?

What is electrical resistance? How is it related to electrical conductivity? How can electrical conductivity and electrical resistance be measured?

Why is it dangerous to touch electrical devices connected to household electricity with wet hands? **Do not try it!** Do some library research to find the answer.

5

Magic Through Motion

The experiments in this chapter have to do with things that move or do not move when you expect them to. All motion can be explained by three fundamental laws established by Isaac Newton in the seventeenth century. The first law states that an object in motion or at rest keeps moving or remains at rest unless a force acts on it. (The force that acts on moving objects is commonly friction.)

The second law has to do with what happens when a force *is* applied to an object. For anything to change its motion or start moving, a force has to act on it. That force (a push or pull) can be one that you exert with your muscles, or it can be the force of gravity, electricity, magnetism, or the forces within the nuclei of atoms. Whenever a force does act on an object (provided that force can overcome friction), the object accelerates. That is, its velocity increases with time. However, unless a force is very large, it must act for a reasonable length of time to produce significant motion. In several of the experiments that follow, the time that the force acts is very small. As a result, the motion you might expect to see never occurs.

The second law also states that the acceleration a body acquires when a force acts on it depends on its mass. The larger the mass, the greater the force that is needed to provide a certain acceleration.

The third law states that when one object pushes on a second, the second object pushes back on the first with a force that is equal but in the opposite direction. You push down on the floor with a force equal to your weight. The floor pushes up on you with an equal force.

5-1*
The Switch and Twist

Your audience sees two lead sinkers on strings that hang below a screen that hides the upper ends of the strings, as shown in Figure 27a. The paper screen used to hide the upper ends of the strings is taped to a board that rests on the seat of the chair and extends out beyond the strings and the weights suspended from them. Pull one of the lead sinkers to the side and release it. It swings back and forth like a pendulum (which it is), but it slowly transfers its motion to the other lead sinker and stops as the motion of the other sinker increases. Then the second sinker's motion diminishes as its energy is transferred back to the first sinker.

Things you will need:
- 2 lead sinkers
- string
- drinking straw or stick
- paper screen to hide strings
- tape
- chair
- board

After several transfers of motion, you might say, "It seems as though only one will dance at a time. Let's see if we can change that." You make an adjustment behind the screen and again pull one of the two lead sinkers aside and release it. This time the two "dancers" move together, but their back-and-forth motion changes from back-and-forth to a "twist."

The Science Behind the Magic

Figure 27b shows the two lead sinkers without the screen. As you can see, the strings leading to the lead weights are connected by a drinking straw or stick at a point about halfway between the weights and the points where the strings are taped to the chair. Each string is wrapped around the straw or stick once. The straw or stick connecting the strings allows energy to be transferred from one swinging weight to the other. To change the motion from back-and-forth to the "twist," the stick is moved closer to the weights.

100

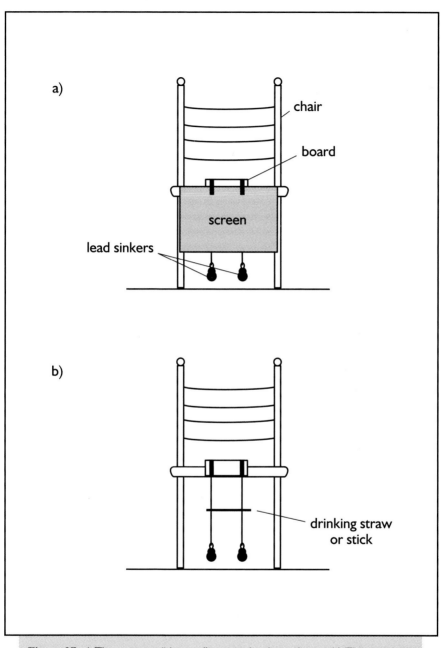

a)

chair

board

screen

lead sinkers

b)

drinking straw
or stick

Figure 27. a) The swinging "dancers" as seen by the audience. b) The apparatus without the screen that hides the straw or stick connecting the strings.

Exploring on Your Own

Try to explain why both lead sinkers move when the straw connector is placed closer to the weights. Explain, too, why the motion changes from back-and-forth to a twist.

What happens to the motion if the straw connecting the two strings is not horizontal?

What happens to the motion if the strings are unequal in length?

5-2*
Which Falls Faster, Light or Heavy?

Tell your audience the story of Galileo and the Leaning Tower of Pisa, where Galileo dropped a heavy ball and a light ball. As doubters watched, Galileo demonstrated that the two balls

Things you will need:
- baseball
- tennis ball
- book
- sheet of paper

fell side by side. The skeptics could not believe what they observed because they were certain that heavy objects fell more rapidly than light ones.

After telling the story, you can demonstrate Galileo's experiment by dropping a baseball and a tennis ball from the same height at the same time. The audience will observe that both balls strike the floor at very nearly the same instant.

Hold a book in one hand and a sheet of paper in the other. Release the book and the paper at the same time. The book will reach the floor well before the paper. Then tell the audience that you can make the book and paper fall at the same rate.

Place the paper on the book and release them together, as shown in Figure 28. The paper remains on the book's cover and falls with the book. Then squeeze the paper into a small ball and drop it side by side with the book. They will fall to the floor at very nearly the same rate. In fact, you can then drop the paper ball and the tennis ball or baseball at the same time. They, too, will fall side by side to the floor.

The Science Behind the Magic

In a vacuum, all objects fall at the same rate; that is, their speed increases at a steady rate because they are pulled downward by the force of gravity. Outside a vacuum, air offers resistance to falling objects. It exerts an upward force that opposes gravity in much the same way that friction opposes motion along a horizontal surface.

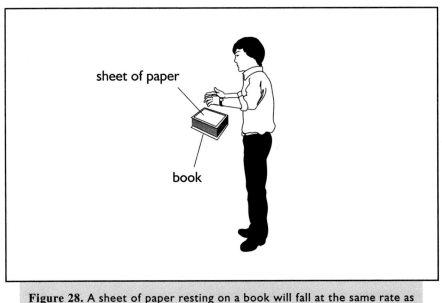

sheet of paper

book

Figure 28. A sheet of paper resting on a book will fall at the same rate as the book.

This upward force, known as air resistance, has a greater effect on light objects than it does on heavy ones. Consequently, in air, a light object will fall at a slower rate than a heavy object of the same size. Since the force of air resistance depends on the surface area of the falling object, an open sheet of paper will fall at a much slower rate than one that has been squeezed into a ball.

Exploring on Your Own

Design and carry out an experiment to find the acceleration of a falling object, such as a lead weight.

What is meant by the *terminal velocity* of a falling object? What factors determine the terminal velocity of an object in air? What is the terminal velocity of a skydiver before his or her parachute opens? What is a skydiver's terminal velocity after his parachute opens?

Newton, a Card, a Marble, and a Bottle

This is a quick and easy scene, but you will need to practice it several times before you attempt it in front of an audience.

Show your audience a glass bottle with a small mouth. Set the bottle on a table and place a small piece of a file card about

Things you will need:

- glass bottle with a small mouth
- table
- piece of a file card about 4 cm x 6 cm (1.5 in x 2.5 in)
- marble with diameter greater than the mouth of the bottle

4 cm x 6 cm (1.5 in x 2.5 in) on the mouth of the bottle. Next, place a marble on the card so that it is centered over the mouth of the bottle. Tell your audience that you will move the card without moving the marble. Then snap a finger against one end of the card (see Figure 29). The card flies away, leaving the marble perched on the mouth of the bottle.

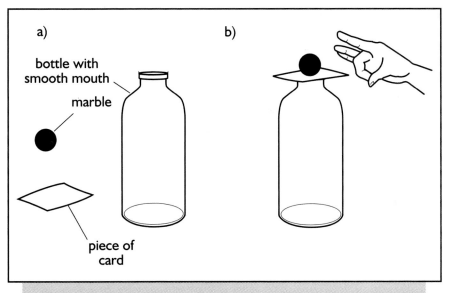

a)

bottle with smooth mouth

marble

piece of card

b)

Figure 29. a) Items needed for the scene. b) Items assembled and ready for action!

The Science Behind the Magic

Newton's first law of motion states that an object maintains its state of motion unless acted upon by an outside force. If it is at rest, as is the case in this scene, it remains at rest. Of course, the card, as it slides out from under the marble, exerts a small force on the marble. However, the frictional force between the card and the marble is small, and it acts for a very short time because you snap the card away quickly with your finger. If the force acts for a longer time, it can move the marble off the bottle. You can see that this is true by pulling the card out slowly from under the marble.

5-4*
Newton, a Table, a Cloth, and a Glass of Water

This scene should follow or be used as a substitute for the previous one. It is also based on Newton's first law of motion.

Things you will need:
- plastic sheet
- small, smooth-surfaced table
- plastic cup
- water
- stone
- plate
- silverware
- teacup and saucer

Use a plastic sheet as a tablecloth on a smooth table. Put a plastic cup half filled with water on the plastic. Tell your audience that you will remove the "tablecloth" without lifting or disturbing the cup of water. You proceed to grasp one side of the tablecloth and quickly jerk it from beneath the cup of water.

You will have to practice this scene several times before you perform it in front of an audience. You have to pull the plastic very quickly so as not to disturb the cup. You will find that lifting the plastic and then pulling it quickly down and out works best. To avoid spills, it is wise to try this experiment first with a cup that holds a stone rather than water. Once you have confidence in your ability to pull the cover off quickly, you can try it with a water-filled cup. Later, as your confidence grows, you might add a plate, silverware, and a teacup and saucer. Such an assortment will make the scene more impressive.

The Science Behind the Magic

This act is another illustration of Newton's first law of motion. It also reveals the importance of the time that a force is applied. The product of force and time ($F \times t$) is called impulse. When an impulse acts on an object, the object acquires momentum, which is equal to its mass times its velocity ($m \times v$). If the force is large but the time very short, the momentum acquired by the object on which the force acts will be small. In this experiment, you strive to make the time that the plastic pulls on the cup as small as possible. In that way, the cup's momentum will remain very close to zero.

Exploring on Your Own

Design your own demonstration to show that a body in motion maintains its velocity unless acted on by an outside force.

5-5*
Which Falls Faster, an Object Projected or Dropped?

Things you will need:

- 2 coins
- 30-cm (1-ft) rigid ruler
- table
- 2 marbles

Ask your audience which will fall to the floor faster from the same height, an object that is dropped straight down or an object that is projected outward horizontally like a bullet shot from a gun. Most people think that an object that falls straight down will reach the floor first because it does not travel as far.

Once they have made their predictions, you can show them that both objects reach the floor at the same time. You can do this in one of two ways, or in both ways if you prefer. As shown in Figure 30a, hold a ruler near a table edge with your index finger. One coin rests on the outer end of the ruler; the other, on the table by the inner end. Hit the ruler sharply with your free hand at the point indicated by the arrow. The coin resting on the ruler will fall straight down to the floor as the ruler moves out from under it. The coin on the table will be projected horizontally. Listen carefully. Do the two coins hit the floor at the same time, or does one land before the other?

Alternatively, you can support two large marbles between your thumb and index finger, as shown in Figure 30b. Snap one finger of your other hand against one of the marbles to project it horizontally. Since contact between the two marbles is holding them in place, if one is sent off in a horizontal direction, the other will fall. Listen carefully as soon as the two marbles begin their different paths to the floor. Do the two marbles hit the floor at the same time, or does one land before the other?

The Science Behind the Magic

Galileo demonstrated about four hundred years ago that the vertical motion of an object, which is the result of gravity pulling the object

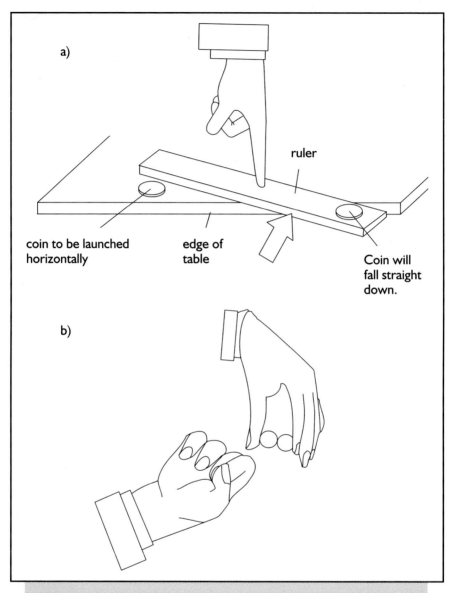

a)

ruler

coin to be launched
horizontally

edge of
table

Coin will
fall straight
down.

b)

Figure 30. To demonstrate that an object that is launched horizontally falls at the same rate as one that falls vertically, you can: a) Use a ruler to send one coin horizontally from a tabletop at the same time another falls vertically. To do so, strike the ruler sharply at the point indicated by the arrow; b) Use a snap of your finger to launch one marble horizontally at the same time another marble starts its downward fall. In either case, you will hear both objects strike the floor at the same time.

to the earth, is independent of any horizontal motion. The vertical acceleration caused by a gravitational force is the same whether or not an object has horizontal motion.

Exploring on Your Own

Design and carry out an experiment to map the path followed by an object that is launched horizontally from a height such as the top of a table. What is the shape of the path? Does the shape of the path depend on the height from which the object is launched?

A Small Force Can Beat a Big Force

Ask the biggest and strongest member of the audience to come forward. Tell your audience that with just one finger, you can prevent this strong person from placing the end of a broom handle on a small target, such as a coaster, that you place on the floor.

Things you will need:
- strong person
- broom with long handle
- small object, such as a coaster, to serve as a target

Hand the strong person the broom and tell him or her to hold the broomstick with both hands next to its straw part, as shown in Figure 31. Then place just one finger on the side of the broomstick near the end.

target

Figure 31. A big force can be counterbalanced by a small one if the distance from the fulcrum is large enough.

When both of you are ready, tell the person holding the broom to try to place the end of the broom handle on the target. He or she will find the task impossible. With just one finger you can control the broomstick and prevent it from being placed on the target.

The Science Behind the Magic

The broom handle is a lever. The fulcrum of this lever is the strong person's lower hand. That person's upper hand is very close to the fulcrum, while your finger is much farther from the fulcrum. The product of a force and its distance from the fulcrum is defined as a "moment of force." Suppose the strong person exerts a force of 500 newtons (110 lbs) at a point 10 cm (4 in) from the fulcrum. If your finger is 100 cm (1.0 m) from the fulcrum, you need to provide a force of only 50 newtons (11 lbs) to counterbalance the larger force. Your moment of force will then balance that of the stronger person.

$$500 \text{ N} \times 0.1 \text{ m} = 50 \text{ N} \times 1.0 \text{ m}$$

If you would like, you can show your audience that if you let the strong person move his lower hand (the fulcrum) down the broom handle, you will no longer be able to control the position of the broomstick.

Exploring on Your Own

Who was Archimedes? What did he discover about levers? What else did he discover?

Use the moment-of-force principle to build a balance that can measure very small objects, such as an insect or a grain of sand.

5-7*
An Upside-Down Pail of Water That Does Not Spill

It is best to practice this bit of science magic outside until you have perfected it.

Tell your audience that you can make water stay in a pail

that is upside down. Then pour some water into a plastic pail. Pour a few drops from the pail so they can see that the pail definitely contains water. No trickery is involved.

Then proceed to swing the pail in a vertical circle. The lower end of the diameter of the circle, as shown in Figure 32, is at a point where the pail would normally hang from your hand when your arm is at your side. The upper end of the diameter of the circular path is well above your head at a point where the pail would be if your arm were raised as high as possible. Despite the fact that the pail is upside down when at the top of the vertical circle through which you swing it, no water falls from the pail.

The Science Behind the Magic

The water stays in the pail for the same reason that passengers on a loop-the-loop roller coaster do not fall from their seats. Newton's second law of motion states that when a force acts on an object, that object accelerates in the direction of the force. The greater the force, the greater the acceleration.

To make an object (the pail in this case) move in a circle, there has to be a force pulling inward on the object. This force, F, produces an inward (centripetal) acceleration, a, which is equal to the square of the object's velocity divided by the radius of the circle (v^2/r). The water remains in the pail because of the centripetal force you exert on the pail. The force with which you pull on the pail is always inward, toward the center of the vertical circle through which the pail moves. (At the top of the circle, that force is downward.) If

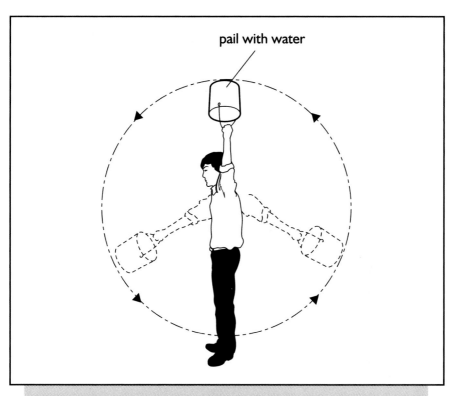

Figure 32. You can keep water in an upside-down pail if you swing the pail in a vertical circle.

the centripetal acceleration is greater than the acceleration due to gravity (the acceleration with which objects fall to the earth), then the water will stay in the pail.

Suppose you swing the pail through a circle that has a radius of one meter (m) at a rate of one swing per second. The velocity of the bottom of the pail will be equal to the circumference of the circle (π x diameter) divided by one second.

$$\pi \times \text{diameter}/1.0 \text{ s} = 3.14 \times 2 \text{ m}/1.0 \text{ s} = 6.28 \text{ m/s}$$

The acceleration of the bottom of the pail will be

$$v^2/r = (6.28 \text{ m/s})^2 /1.0 \text{ m} = 39.4 \text{ m/s}^2.$$

Since this acceleration is more than four times the acceleration due to gravity, which is 9.8 m/s^2, the water remains in the pail.

Exploring on Your Own

What is the difference between a centripetal force and a centrifugal force? Why is a centrifugal force often called a "fictitious" force?

Watch a roller coaster that does a loop. Make some estimates to determine the radius of the loop and the speed of the car that carries passengers. From your estimates, determine the centripetal acceleration of the car at the top of the loop. How does the car's centripetal acceleration compare with the acceleration due to gravity?

5-8*
The Magic Yardstick

Things you will need:

• yardstick

• clay

Place a yardstick on your index fingers, as shown in Figure 33a. Both hands should be close to opposite ends of the yardstick. Ask your audience where on the yardstick your hands will meet if you slide them together slowly beneath the yardstick. Most will say that your hands will meet in the middle (under the 18-inch line), and they will be right.

Now place the yardstick so that one hand is under the 3-inch line and the other is under the 24-inch line, as shown in Figure 33b. Ask the audience where they think your hands will meet this time. Most will probably predict that the stick will fall off the finger that is under the 24-inch line. But when you do move your hands, they again meet under the 18-inch line.

Next, place a lump of clay near one end of the yardstick and your fingers under the yardstick near each end, as shown in Figure 33c. Where does your audience think your hands will meet now?

When you actually slide your hands under the yardstick, they meet at a point somewhere between the middle of the yardstick and the lump of clay. The exact point will depend on the weight of the clay.

The Science Behind the Magic

There is friction between your fingers and the yardstick. The frictional force depends on the weight pressing against your fingers. The greater the weight, the greater the friction. In the first case, the weight on each finger is approximately equal and remains that way when you slide them until they meet at the middle of the yardstick. The center of the yardstick is also its center of gravity—the point where all the weight can be considered to be and the point where the stick can be lifted without it rotating.

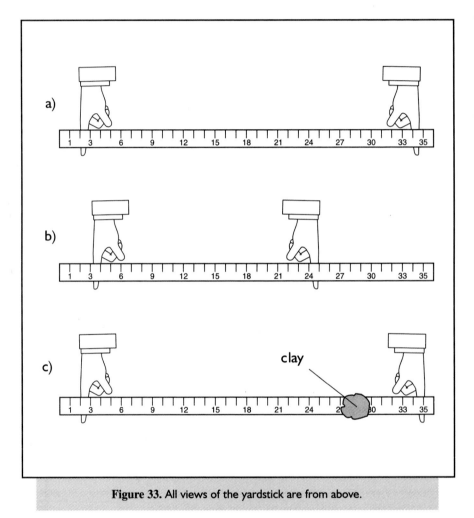

Figure 33. All views of the yardstick are from above.

In the second case, there is more weight on the finger closer to the center of the stick. Consequently, there is more friction between that finger and the stick. As a result, the hand near the end of the stick moves approximately nine inches before the weight on the two hands becomes equal. Then both hands slide to the 18-inch line.

In the third case, a weight is placed near one end of the yard-stick. The finger near the weighted end, therefore, has more weight on it than the one near the unweighted end. The added weight means more friction; consequently, it is the finger near the unweighted end that slides until the weight on it matches the weight on the other finger.

The point where the hands meet this time is the new center of gravity, the center of gravity for the stick and the clay.

Exploring on Your Own

How is this experiment related to moments of force, which you encountered in Experiment 5-6?

In addition to weight, what other factors affect the friction between two surfaces?

5-9
The Start-Again Stop-Again Jar

Place a half-filled jar of honey or molasses on a wide board that serves as a ramp. Use a block of wood or a book to raise one end of the board, as shown in Figure 34. Instead of rolling down the ramp as the audience would expect, the jar stops and then starts again in stop-and-go fashion until it reaches the bottom of the ramp.

Things you will need:

- round half-filled jar of honey or molasses
- wide board
- block of wood or a book

If, in practicing this scene, the jar rolls down the ramp at a steady speed, the slope of the ramp is too steep. Reduce the slope until the jar moves in a stop-and-go fashion.

Since a substance becomes thinner (less viscous) as its temperature rises, you may need to warm or cool the honey or molasses to obtain the best results.

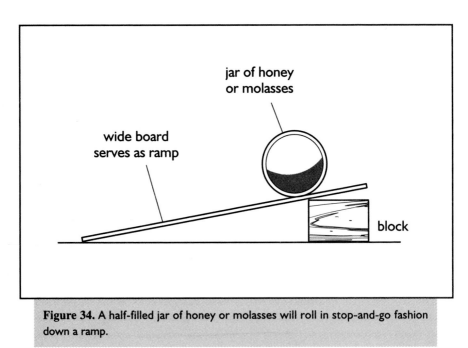

jar of honey
or molasses

wide board
serves as ramp

block

Figure 34. A half-filled jar of honey or molasses will roll in stop-and-go fashion down a ramp.

The Science Behind the Magic

The honey in the jar is very thick (viscous). As the jar starts to roll, some of the honey sticks to the upward side of the jar. This moves the weight farther back, producing a force that prevents the downward movement of the jar caused by gravity. Slowly, the honey slides back down the side of the jar until the net force caused by the weight of the honey causes it to again roll a short distance down the ramp.

List of Suppliers

The following companies supply the materials that may be needed for science fair projects:

Carolina Biological Supply Co.
2700 York Road
Burlington, NC 27215
(800) 334-5551
http://www.carolina.com

Central Scientific Co. (CENCO)
3300 Cenco Parkway
Franklin Park, IL 60131
(800) 262-3626
http://www.cenconet.com

**Connecticut Valley Biological
Supply Co., Inc.**
82 Valley Road, Box 326
Southampton, MA 01073
(800) 628-7748

Delta Education
P.O. Box 915
Hudson, NH 03051-0915
(800) 258-1302

Edmund Scientific Co.
101 East Gloucester Pike
Barrington, NJ 08007
(609) 547-3488

Fisher Science Education
485 S. Frontage Road
Burr Ridge, IL 60521
(800) 955-1177
http://www.fisheredu.com/

Frey Scientific
100 Paragon Parkway
Mansfield, OH 44905
(800) 225-3739

Nasco-Fort Atkinson
P.O. Box 901
Fort Atkinson, WI 53538-0901
(800) 558-9595

Nasco-Modesto
P.O. Box 3837
Modesto, CA 95352-3837
(800) 558-9595
http://www.nasco.com

Sargent-Welch/VWR Scientific
P.O. Box 5229
Buffalo Grove, IL 60089-5229
(800) SAR-GENT
http://www.SargentWelch.com

**Science Kit & Boreal
Laboratories**
777 East Park Drive
Tonawanda, NY 14150
(800) 828-7777
http://sciencekit.com

Ward's Natural Science Establishment, Inc.
P.O. Box 92912
Rochester, NY 14692-9012
(800) 962-2660
http://www.wardsci.com

Further Reading

Adams, Richard, and Robert Gardner. *Ideas for Science Projects, Revised Edition*. Danbury, Conn.: Franklin Watts, 1997.

———. *More Ideas for Science Projects, Revised Edition*. Danbury, Conn.: Franklin Watts, 1998.

Bochinski, Julianne Blair. *The Complete Handbook of Science Fair Projects*. New York: John Wiley, 1996.

Bombaugh, Ruth. *Science Fair Success, Revised and Expanded*. Springfield, N.J.: Enslow Publishers, Inc., 1999.

Friedhoffer, Robert. *Magic Tricks, Science Facts*. New York: Franklin Watts, 1990.

Gardner, Martin. "Physics Trick of the Month." *The Physics Teacher*, December 1991, p. 587.

Gardner, Robert. *Science Fair Projects—Planning, Presenting, Succeeding*. Springfield, N.J.: Enslow Publishers, Inc., 1999.

———. *What's So Super About the Supernatural?* Millbrook, Conn.: Twenty-First Century Books, The Millbrook Press, 1998.

Herbert, Don. *Mr. Wizard's Experiments for Young Scientists*. New York: Doubleday, 1990.

Hoyt, Marie A. *Work-Game Sheets for Magnet Magic Etc.* New York: Educational Services Press, 1984.

Kenda, Margaret. *Science Wizardry for Kids*. Hauppauge, N.Y.: Barron's Educational Series, Inc., 1995.

Krieger, Melanie Jacobs. *How to Excel in Science Competitions, Revised and Updated*. Springfield, N.J.: Enslow Publishers, Inc., 1999.

Ladizinsky, Eric. *More Magical Science Tricks for Young Scientists*. Los Angeles: Lowell House, 1994.

Markle, Sandra. *The Young Scientist's Guide to Successful Science Projects*. New York: Lothrop, Lee, and Shepard, 1990.

McCarthy, Donald. *More Fun with Science Magic*. Athens, Ohio: University Classics, 1991.

Moorman, Thomas. *How to Make Your Science Project Scientific*. New York: Atheneum, 1975.

Nickell, Joe. *Wonder Workers! How They Perform the Impossible*. Amherst, N.Y.: Prometheus Books, 1992.

Stine, Megan, et al. *Hands-On Science Mystery & Magic*. Milwaukee: Gareth Stevens, Inc., 1993.

Tocci, Salvatore. *How to Do a Science Fair Project, Revised Edition*. Danbury, Conn.: Franklin Watts, 1997.

Van Cleave, Janice. *Two Hundred and One Awesome, Magical, Bizarre, and Incredible Experiments*. New York: John Wiley, 1994.

White, Jr., Laurence B., and Ray Broekel. *Shazam! Simple Science Magic*. Morton Grove, Ill.: A. Whitman, 1991.

Internet Addresses

Gould, Chris. *Science Fairs*. July 12, 1999. <http://physics.usc.edu/~gould/ScienceFairs/> (August 2, 1999).

Holme, Thomas. *Science Fun for Everyone*. n.d. <http://www.uwm.edu/~tholme/fun/main.shtml> (August 2, 1999).

Morano, David. "Experimental Science Projects: An Introductory Level Guide." *Cyber Fair Home Page*. May 27, 1999. <http://www.isd77.k12.mn.us/resources/cf/SciProjIntro.html> (July 30, 1999).

Index

A

acid-base
    indicators, 54–55, 56,
      61–62
    neutralization, 58
    properties, 54–55
air pressure, 11, 14, 53
    to crush a can, 21–22
    and funnel, 15–16
    and geyser, 23, 25
    and leaking bottle, 17–18
    lifting with, 19
    and Ping-Pong ball, 26,
      28
    and submarine, 29–30
air properties, 11–12
air resistance, 103–104
ammonia, 54, 56, 57, 58,
    59–60, 61
angles, 88, 90
    of incidence, 42
    of refraction, 42

B

balloons, 26, 31–32
    in a bottle, 13–14
Bernoulli's principle, 26, 28
bicarbonate, 58
bleach, 65
blind spot, 38–39
bloody hand, 57
blue bottle, 73–74

C

carbon dioxide, 58

center of gravity, 117, 119
centripetal force, 114–116
chemical magic, 50–58, 62–66
    and color, 59–61, 73–74
    invisible ink, 67–70
citric acid, 58
conduction, electrical, 96–97
copper sulfate, 59, 60, 63–64

D

dancing raisins, 51
density, 51, 53, 87
disappearing
    coin, 40, 42
    glass, 86–87
    ink, 65
    letter, 38–39
dragon's blood, 56

F

friction, 103, 117

G

Galileo, 25, 103, 109
gas solubility, 51
genie in a bottle, 53–53
gravity, 109, 111, 115, 116,
    121
    defying, 26, 28, 94–95
    and mass, 103–104

I

illusions, 45–47
impulse, 107

inverted images
  real, 76, 78–79, 83
  shadow, 80, 82
invisible ink, 67–70

J
jumping flame, 71–72

L
laws of motion, 98–99,
  105–108, 114
lead acetate, 59, 60
lead hydroxide, 60
lens, 76, 78–79
  cylindrical, 83, 85
lever, 112–113
litmus paper, 54–55

M
mirrors, 88, 90
moment of force, 113
momentum, 107
mysterious die, 45–46

N
Newton, Isaac, 98
  laws of, 98–99, 105–108,
  114

P
pendulums, 100, 102
persistence of vision, 34,
  36–37
  and television, 37

phenolphthalein, 56, 57, 58, 59,
  60
pressure and balloon radius,
  31–32

R
refraction, 76, 78–79, 83, 85
  index of, 87
reappearing coin, 40, 42

S
safety, 9–10
science fairs, 8–9
seltzer tablets, 58
starch-iodine reaction, 66
steel nail, 63–64
  floating, 91, 93
submarine, 29–30
surface tension, 91, 93

T
terminal velocity, 104

V
vinegar, 56, 61, 93
viscosity, 120–121
vision
  blind spot, 38–39
  and contrast, 48–49
  far and near, 43–44
  persistence of, 34, 36–37
  three-dimensional, 43